T0328666

Cambridge Elements ≡

Elements in Beckett Studies
edited by
Dirk Van Hulle
University of Oxford
Mark Nixon
University of Reading

BECKETT AND CIORAN

Steven Matthews
University of Reading

CAMBRIDGE
UNIVERSITY PRESS

Shaftesbury Road, Cambridge CB2 8EA, United Kingdom

One Liberty Plaza, 20th Floor, New York, NY 10006, USA

477 Williamstown Road, Port Melbourne, VIC 3207, Australia

314–321, 3rd Floor, Plot 3, Splendor Forum, Jasola District Centre, New Delhi – 110025, India

103 Penang Road, #05–06/07, Visioncrest Commercial, Singapore 238467

Cambridge University Press is part of Cambridge University Press & Assessment, a department of the University of Cambridge.

We share the University's mission to contribute to society through the pursuit of education, learning and research at the highest international levels of excellence.

www.cambridge.org
Information on this title: www.cambridge.org/9781009494724

DOI: 10.1017/9781009351560

© Steven Matthews 2024

This publication is in copyright. Subject to statutory exception and to the provisions of relevant collective licensing agreements, no reproduction of any part may take place without the written permission of Cambridge University Press & Assessment.

When citing this work, please include a reference to the DOI 10.1017/9781009351560

First published 2024

A catalogue record for this publication is available from the British Library

ISBN 978-1-009-49472-4 Hardback
ISBN 978-1-009-35155-3 Paperback
ISSN 2632-0746 (online)
ISSN 2632-0738 (print)

Cambridge University Press & Assessment has no responsibility for the persistence or accuracy of URLs for external or third-party internet websites referred to in this publication and does not guarantee that any content on such websites is, or will remain, accurate or appropriate.

Beckett and Cioran

Elements in Beckett Studies

DOI: 10.1017/9781009351560
First published online: March 2024

Steven Matthews
University of Reading
Author for correspondence: Steven Matthews, s.matthews@reading.ac.uk

Abstract: This Element discusses the association between Samuel Beckett and the Romanian-born philosopher E. M. Cioran. It draws upon the known biographical detail, but, more substantially, upon the terms of Beckett's engagement with Cioran's writings from the 1950s to the 1970s. Certain of Cioran's key conceptualisations, such as that of the 'meteque', and his version of philosophical scepticism resonate with aspects of Beckett's writing as it evolved beyond the 'siege in the room'. More particularly, aspects of Cioran's conclusion about the formal nature that philosophy must assume chime with some of the formal decisions taken by Beckett in the mid-late prose. Through close reading of some of Beckett's key works such as *Texts for Nothing* and *How It Is*, and through consideration of Beckett's choices when translating between English and French, the issues of identity and understanding shared by these two settlers in Paris are mutually illuminated.

This Element also has a video abstract: www.cambridge.org/EIBS_Matthews

Keywords: Beckett, E. M. Cioran, philosophy, scepticism, pessimism

© Steven Matthews 2024

ISBNs: 9781009494724 (HB), 9781009351553 (PB), 9781009351560 (OC)
ISSNs: 2632-0746 (online), 2632-0738 (print)

Contents

Introduction

There are many parallels and affinities between the work of Samuel Beckett and that of the Romanian-born philosopher E. M. Cioran (1911–95). Yet awareness of Cioran within Beckett Studies has been notably limited, often dependent upon Cioran's memoir 'Beckett: Quelques Recontres' [Beckett: Some Meetings] (1974), which was eventually collected in Cioran's late volume *Aveux et anathèmes* (1987). In that book, the recollection of Beckett appears amongst a notably eclectic constellation of admired international writers and thinkers, including Cioran's fellow Romanian Mircea Eliade, Henri Michaux, Roger Caillois, Alexis Léger Saint-John Perse, F. Scott Fitzgerald, Maria Zambrano, and Jorge Luis Borges. In this context, Cioran's admiring portrait of Beckett has wide resonance: a solitary ascetic figure, seemingly detached from the world around him, yet one oddly comfortable, perhaps at home, in Paris. This is a Beckett fretting continually about language and linguistic possibility, monkish, his presence a bit like that of Wittgenstein or of a Buddhist. The conversations that Cioran reports he had with Beckett are about Joyce and Swift; Cioran demonstrates that he knows Beckett's book on Proust, *Malone Dies*, and that Beckett has been translating the prose aphorisms of the eighteenth-century writer Chamfort surprisingly into poetry in English (Cioran, 2011, 1191–5).

All of this of course chimes with a demotic sense which has sustained currency, a demotic sense of Beckett as a person and consequently as a writer. As Emilie Morin suggests, through quoting a phrase from Cioran on Beckett in the opening paragraph of her *Beckett's Political Imagination*, such a portrait as that Cioran draws in 'Some Meetings' establishes a kind of signal consensus view – and it is one to be resisted, as her compelling and detailed argument on behalf of a more engaged and aware Beckett eloquently does (Morin, 2017, 1). Yet, and also, from even the bald description just given, Cioran's version of Beckett is hectic and dishevelled in comparison to the 'separate' figure of the subject he otherwise creates. This is particularly so around the issue of 'origins', which Cioran claims we can all no longer have, so that it is equally important and wholly unimportant, for example, that Beckett is Irish (Cioran, 2011, 1194). On this ambiguity and other grounds, Cioran's portrait of Beckett in 'Some Meetings', as well as being taken for a representative, even definitive portrayal of a uniquely otherworldly, noble, and saintly figure, deserves to be read comparatively against the spectrum of Cioran's other engagements with Beckett himself.

More importantly, this 'Some Meetings' portrait should be placed alongside Cioran's philosophical writings, particularly as they developed in the years after the Second World War. The affinities and shared preoccupations between the two writers, in other words, deserve further exploration, as this Element under-takes, the better to understand those aspects of each writer's work which particularly appealed, or which set resonances sounding between them. This Element is not, therefore, a study of influence, of that of Cioran upon Beckett, for instance. Both writers had established trajectories before they became aware of each other's work. Rather, this Element seeks to trace some lines of the dialogue which clearly existed between the two. These lines ran through personal connection, and as both were writers and readers of each other. Their dialogue illuminates important moments in the development of their evolving thinking about their work, and also reveals much within the Parisian context that Beckett and Cioran shared from the later war years, through, severally, to their deaths.

The personal encounters between Beckett and Cioran through the 1960s and 1970s were largely casual – meetings in the Paris streets, for late-night drinks, at some dinner parties, even occasional visits to and dinners at the Becketts' apartment. Beckett and Cioran each sent the other copies of their work on publication from the 1960s onwards. It is of course impossible to recover the substance of their conversation beyond what 'Some Meetings' recounts. It is also impossible to recover a material sense of what each knew of the other's lives before they first met – an important issue, as we shall see, with regard to Cioran's association with the Fascist group in Romania before the War.

This Element will seek to recover the traceable facts about the personal relationship. It will also trace the affinities in the thinking and writing of Beckett and Cioran as they developed, once both had adopted French as their predominant language as writers in the post-War years. There are affinities in the ways that their engagement with that post-War moment led both Beckett and Cioran to pursue a more broken, fragmented form in their work, an interrupted form that was also echoed in the content of that writing – a shared preoccupation with alienated identities, exiles, and refugees, and with ruined, even post-apocalyptic landscapes. In the process of this development too, we find that in both authors, the attitude of the writing towards its audience shifts, becomes more intransigent in its refusal to accommodate the reader, even violent in its refusals in that regard.

To this end, Section 1 of this Element will document the known relationship between Beckett and Cioran, pointing out the inadequacies in the extant biograph-ical accounts. It will consider both writers as outsiders in post-War Paris, and the virtues which particularly Cioran came to perceive in that situation. Cioran's controversial self-characterisation as a 'métèque', a non-autochthonous resident alongside native inhabitants, will be placed alongside the complex identifications of the personae in Beckett's *Texts for Nothing* as shared responses to the immediate post-War moment. The French original of *Texts* will be weighed alongside Beckett's translation of it into English, to reveal the different inflections which enter as Beckett reconsiders some of the key notes for different readers. Section 2 of this Element will pursue the underpinnings of the growing alteration in both Beckett's and Cioran's work by thinking through Beckett's early understanding of philosophy, as figured in his *'Philosophy Notes'* of the 1930s. This is in order to consider the shared perspective upon the history of Cioran's discipline that Beckett had when meeting Cioran. The philosophical pessimism and scepticism in both writers' response to their circumstance informs the formal shapes their work increasingly adopts. The section will discuss Beckett's *Fizzles* in this regard, alongside some of Beckett's 1970s poems, as the discussion further takes up some shared interests in French and English authors of the eighteenth century.

What the philosophical debate in Section 2 tends towards is an increasing characterisation of that formal and content-led aspect of both Beckett's and Cioran's later writings – interest in the fragment and the aphorism as the proper shape truly sceptical work must assume. Section 3 considers this conclusion against Beckett's *Comment C'est/How It Is*, presenting the confrontational nature of this text in its understanding of historical change. A brief coda to the Element then turns to Paul Celan, a fellow Romanian and an acquaintance and translator of Cioran, to provide a final reflection upon the formal possibilities that these non-French dwellers in Paris increasingly explored and shared across the latter part of their writing careers.

1 'Great stuff here and there' – Beckett and Cioran Together

1.1 Dinners and Phonecalls – Personal Connections

In April 1970, E. M. Cioran attended Jack MacGowran's solo performance of selections from Samuel Beckett's work in Paris. Cioran noted in his daybook, later published in edited form as *Cahiers 1957–1972*, that he was 'frappé' [struck] by the experience: 'J'ai été frappé par les affinités qui existent entre la Weltanschauung de Sam et la mienne. Fondementalement, la même impossibilité d'être' (Cioran, 1997, 803).[1]

---

[1] 'I was taken aback by the similarities which exist between Sam's world view and my own. Basically, the same impossibility of being.' All translations in this discussion are my own unless otherwise indicated. Thomas Cousineau has provided translations of what he called some of the 'more memorable' passages from Cioran's *Cahiers* regarding Beckett – but this passage, amongst several other important accounts of meeting with Beckett or reflecting upon his works, is not included (Cousineau, 2005, 5). Cioran published a brief article, 'Beckett ou l'Horreur d'être né', in response to the MacGowran evening – a stepping stone to Cioran's next work, *L'inconvenient d'être né*, with which he was struggling at the time. The editors of Cioran's *Oeuvres* imply that his

Beckett and Cioran were both personal and respectful regarding each other's writing. The two seemingly first met at the Closerie des Lilas on 8 January 1956 (Cioran, 2011, 1579).[2] As evidenced from Cioran's *Cahiers*, memoirs, and interviews, and from Beckett's correspondence, many encounters followed, by chance and otherwise, in the boulevards, Luxembourg Gardens, through dinners, and late-night drinks sessions planned and unplanned. Beckett himself told Barbara Bray that he was encountering Cioran frequently in local stores and streets in the early 1960s (Van Hulle and Nixon, 2013, 169). These various encounters extended actively at least until February 1975, when Beckett mentions a recent phone call from Cioran in a letter to someone else.[3] Typically, the call had obviously touched on mutually interesting topics, as Cioran is reported to have urged Beckett, soon to travel to Germany to oversee the Schiller Theater production of *Warten auf Godot*, to make sure to visit the site of Kleist's suicide (Beckett, 2016b, 391).[4] The connection then continues, perhaps at a less intense level, nearly up to Beckett's death. The Beckett Digital Manuscript Project (hereafter the BDMP) confirms that Beckett's library contained new editions of Cioran's work, personally signed to both Beckett and Suzanne, dated as late as 1986 (Beckett, 2016a).

The BDMP catalogue of the library perhaps also confirms what is suggested in Beckett's correspondence – that he was at least somewhat familiar with Cioran's first works written in French from just after the Second World War.[5] The library contains a 1949 (and presumably first) edition of *Précis de décomposition*, a 1960 edition of *Histoire et utopie*, and a 1961 edition of *La tentation d'exister*. Yet Beckett had already recommended *La tentation* in a letter of late November 1956 ('great stuff here and there'), suggesting that he had read the book shortly after its publication (Beckett, 2011, 678). In the same letter, Beckett tells himself that he must reread *Précis*. Then, in June 1960,

---

attendance at the performance enabled Cioran to see how he might write his own text, spurred by some of the more aphoristic phrases in Beckett's work (Cioran, 2011, 1485).

[2] There seems some ambiguity around what constitutes 'meeting' here – Anthony Cronin's biography, partly reflecting Cioran's memory of it, gives the date as 1961 (Cronin, 1997, 563).

[3] James Knowlson suggests that a distancing between Beckett and Cioran occurred across the later 1970s, as Beckett 'had less in common with Cioran in terms of outlook than he had at first thought' (Knowlson, 1996, 654).

[4] Ackerley and Gontarski report that Beckett had visited the Kleist monument in 1969 (Ackerley and Gontarski, 2004, 299). André Bernold suggests that Beckett knew little of Kleist's writing beyond the essay on the marionette theatre, but that he ploughed through a German book about Kleist in the early 1980s. In 1982, though, Beckett apparently told Bernold that he wished one of his short plays might be performed by marionettes (Bernold, 2015, 73–4, 76–7). As we shall see, Kleist forms a shared influence for Beckett, Cioran, and Celan.

[5] Cioran published three books before he left Romania; their titles translated into English as *On the Heights of Despair* (1934), the politically controversial *Romania's Transfiguration* (1936), and *Tears and Saints* (1937) (Zarifopol-Johnston, 2009, xxi).

Beckett suggested to Bray that a selection of passages from these two Cioran books would be 'well worth' making for the journal *X: A Quarterly Review* (Beckett, 2014, 336). Once Beckett's personal acquaintance with Cioran had become established, he continued warmly to endorse each new work as he looked it over on publication, not least in comments to Cioran himself. In 1969, Beckett wrote from Ussy mentioning the 'pleasure' that all of Cioran's books had brought him; the new one, *Le mauvais démiurge*, included: 'In your ruins I feel at ease' (Beckett, 2016b, 157). In 1973, *De l'inconvénient d'être né* is greeted as a further work that hits straight home; Beckett tells Cioran that he will return often to this 'voix fraternelle' [brotherly voice] (Beckett, 2016b, 348).[6]

And that 'brotherly' listening continued across this decade and more for Cioran too. For instance, late in *Cahiers*, in a passage from early November 1972, Cioran mentions running into Beckett at midnight in the street; they went to the Closerie for several hours, during which Beckett showed 'youthful passion' and excitement when describing his latest work, *Not I*. Then, three days later in the daybook, Cioran comes back to the subject: 'Le *moi*, violà l'obstacle. Je n'arrive pas à le franchir. J'y suis rivé, incurablement' [The *I*, that's the obstacle. I can't succeed in getting past it. I'm nailed to it, incurably] (Cioran, 1997, 996–7). The agony of the speaker in Beckett's play is translated directly into the crucified, self-perceptive, self-commiserating awareness of Cioran.

Given these several documented affinities between Beckett and Cioran, including those perceived, as we shall see, in contemporary debates from the late 1960s onwards, it is somewhat surprising that there has been relatively little commentary to date drawing the two writers together. Benjamin Keatinge laid out many of the grounds and reasons for undertaking what he conceived of as a 'comparative study' of the two writers in 2013, as well as delineating the 'lack' of such a thing in the multiple publications on Beckett where it might have been expected (Keatinge, 2013, 155, 157). Yet that more extended comparison has not emerged, licensing the study here. Moreover, where Beckett *is* admitted to discussions about Cioran, as suggested earlier in this Element, it is often through unquestioning repetition of the latter's autobiographical accounts

---

[6] Cioran's dedication of the copy of this text registered on the BDMP tells Beckett and Suzanne that in it he had tried and failed to write something that might be 'lu par concierges' [read by concierges] (Beckett, 2016a). The projected audience given here cites one of the perverse aphorisms later in *L'inconvenient*, which suggests that it is better for a writer to stick to a single idiom and that more is to be got by 'bavarder avec une concierge' [chatting with a concierge] than speaking to a learned person in another language (Cioran 2011, 867). The dedication might be taken as a shared wish for assimilation, although Cioran's sense here of 'tried but failed' also suggests a continuing sense of the difficulties involved, which will form much of the subject of this Element.

such as his piece 'Samuel Beckett: Some Meetings' – accounts which Cioran's *Cahiers* shows actually to have displeased Beckett, much to Cioran's 'despair' (Cioran, 1997, 810; Farrugia, 2015, 214).[7]

As Keatinge's suggestive piece indicates, however, such approaches founded on biography imply at least some sense of mutual influence on very tenuous grounds; what a study of Beckett and Cioran *together* can hope to achieve is simply to map out those 'conjunctions' which exist, and which can be enlightening for more informed future studies of either writer (Keatinge, 2013, 169). Further to Keatinge's point, such 'conjunctions' also have something to say about the historical situation out of which both authors wrote and of which both were sensitively aware. Consideration of the 'conjunctions' between Beckett and Cioran provides nuanced context for their very similar writerly choices, as we shall see. What was it, in other words, that led Beckett to read *La tentation* soon after publication, to recommend it, at least in part, as 'great stuff', and to set himself enthusiastically to remember to reread *Précis de décomposition*?[8]

The issue of response to historical circumstance is integral to the moment when Beckett's name was becoming more firmly linked to Cioran's internationally, as the latter's work began to be translated into English in the United States. Susan Sontag's 1967 essay, '"Thinking against Oneself": Reflections on Cioran', had originally appeared as the 'Introduction' to Richard Howard's version of *The Temptation to Exist*. The essay gained perhaps greater currency when Sontag included it in her 1969 collection *Styles of Radical Will*. Garnished with an epigraph from Beckett's 'Three Dialogues', above one from the American composer John Cage, Sontag's essay places Cioran within a European tradition of thinkers including Hegel, Kleist, and Nietzsche. For Cioran, she argues, the 'mind is a voyeur' of itself, not of the world. Here, 'to a degree reminiscent of Beckett', Cioran's writings are 'concerned with the absolute integrity of thought. That is, with the reduction or circumspection of

---

[7] Cioran's response to Beckett's displeasure, as relayed by Suzanne, was typically to discuss it with further friends in exile such as Henri Michaux, as *Cahiers* attests. In this instance, Cioran, as often, contrasted Beckett to Nietzsche's 'ridiculous' 'surhomme', recognising the authentic 'misère' of Beckett's characters who 'ne vivent pas dans le tragique mais dans l'incurable' [who don't live amongst the tragic but amongst the incurable] (Cioran, 1997, 810).

[8] It is important too that, when proposing to Bray that a selection of passages from Cioran be made in 1960, Beckett said that he found Cioran's 'aphorismes less interesting' than his essays: neither *Précis*, *La tentation*, or 1960's *Histoire et utopie* contained that section of aphorisms Cioran later included in his book publications. Beckett was perhaps also familiar, then, with the *Syllogismes d'amertume*, which Gallimard had published in 1952. Since both writers were knowledgeable or enthusiastic about earlier French aphorists, including La Rochefoucauld and Chamfort, as we shall see, Beckett's alertness to and weighing of Cioran's achievements in the genre resonate inevitably with aspects of his own achievement.

thought to thinking about thinking' (Cioran, 1968, 14; Sontag, 1969, 80).[9] After delineating a fuller version of this sense of intentness upon the process and mechanisms of thought, Sontag's essay is notable, however, for the way it questions Cioran's politics. She accuses Cioran of 'moral insensitivity' in his thinking about the twentieth-century history of the Jews in the essay 'A People of Solitaries' in *The Temptation* – an essay which falls 'well below Cioran's usual standard of [. . .] perspicacity'. Sontag, as a result, categorises his as a 'right-wing "Catholic" sensibility' and him as a 'conservative'. For Sontag, Cioran ultimately remains 'confined within the premises of the historicizing consciousness' to which he was born, and was only partially able to 'transvalue' it successfully (Sontag, 1969, 86–7, 94). Cioran is unable, in other words, to achieve the new world freedoms of such as John Cage – the Beckett analogy is seemingly forgotten as Sontag develops her political theme.

On, as it were, his first introduction to anglophone audiences, the topic of Cioran's extremely troubling politics, including his anti-Semitism, is (perhaps intuitively on Sontag's part, perhaps not) to the fore. Cioran's support for Hitler and Nazi ideology in the 1930s and through the Second World War is now uncontested and includes horrifying anti-Semitic outbursts in Romanian (Branco, 2019, 26–31). These views culminate in Cioran's ultranationalist book *Romania's Transfiguration* from 1936 and arguably lie in the background of later works such as the essay which perturbs Sontag.[10]

How far Beckett might have been aware of Cioran's 1930s–40s Fascist associations (which will be considered more fully in the next section), or of his anti-Semitic attitudes, beyond what he would have read in *La tentation*, must remain unclear. Ratifiable knowledge of Cioran's politics was to become prevalent only later in France, at around the time of Cioran's death (and after Beckett's): this after Cioran had allowed *Romania's Transfiguration* to be republished in 1991 in edited form (the chapter principally on the Jews was suppressed) in his native country and language with the fall of the Berlin Wall (Zarifopol-Johnson, 2009, 10). Outside of France, there seems to have been

---

[9] Eugene Thacker's 'Foreword' to Howard's translation underlines the personal association with Beckett, noting that Cioran 'befriended' the 'playwright' in post-War Paris, along with Henri Michaux and Gabriel Marcel (Cioran, 1968, 6).

[10] Matei Caluescu has noted that the book is, though, both a product of and resistant to its own historical moment, claiming that it resists 'the primitive, hysterical anti-Semitism' of contemporary Romanian Fascism in projecting the Jewish people as 'in every sense superior' to the provincial outlook of the Romanians. But, controversially, on this account Cioran sees the Jews as not able to be assimilated to Romanian life (Calusecu, 1996, 206). Caluescu's point is that the later French Cioran seeks to 'unwrite' these early views, but that they also perpetuate themselves (197). This troubling doubleness of thinking essentially marks the anti-Semitic tenor of that later essay 'The People of Solitaries', which seeks to valorise a 'superior' Jewish people as archetypal modern wanderers who have resisted most forms of Western decadence (Cioran, 2011, 317–19).

more awareness of this aspect of Cioran's earlier history before the fame that arrived with his post-War work in French. Cioran's volume of interviews, *Entretiens*, contains a 1970 interview published in Vienna in which he is asked about the Romanian Fascist group the Iron Guard (he denies having been a member), and his right-wing associations were again raised in a 1984 interview for Italy's *Vogue* (Cioran, 1995, 12, 131).[11] The former interview might have informed the situation that produced a self-justificatory letter quoted from Cioran to his brother from 1973 by Zarifopol-Johnston, in which Cioran is outraged at what she calls 'attacks on himself in Parisian literary circles' – attacks which continued in 1979 (Zarifopol-Johnston, 2009, 115). Whether Beckett could have picked something of this up remains a matter for speculation. So far as evidence exists, as we have seen, the contact was, for whatever reason, less intense after about 1975, although Cioran continued to send editions of his writing with dedications to Beckett and Suzanne across the remainder of Beckett's lifetime.

To an extent, this impasse when considering Beckett's knowledge of Cioran's first published attitudes reflects the kinds of more general dilemma which is registered in Sontag's considered and qualified admiration for Cioran's thought. For Sontag, Cioran's writings provide a symptomatic, if politically unacceptable, model for the kinds of dead end in which European intellectualism finds itself during the latter part of the twentieth century, one aware of the intractabilities in which history has placed us, but unable to escape (or 'transvalue') them. As with Beckett's statement about Masson from 'Three Dialogues' – the source of Sontag's epigraph for her essay – Cioran represents a kind of 'anguish of helplessness' amidst 'the ferocious dilemma of expression'. Like Beckett's Masson, nonetheless, and like Beckett himself, Cioran keeps 'wriggling' (Beckett, 1983, 140).

Whatever her deep intuition about Cioran's politics, this Element is centrally concerned to challenge Sontag's sense that Cioran – and his implied coeval Beckett – failed to achieve a new stance towards their time after the War. The formal decisions both took as writers, from their very different perspectives and genres, in themselves constituted such a stance. Formal choice in all writing is always a choice imbued with other actualities. This is so, in Theodor Adorno's sense that formal aesthetics provide a space which produces exemplary reading of the times and thence a political answering-back. With regard to Joyce and Beckett, Adorno claimed that their 'power' resides in their 'immersing themselves totally, monadologically, in the laws of their own forms, laws which are

---

[11] Zarifopol-Johnston also considers this *Vogue* interview and Cioran's confrontation with his reputation in Italy as someone with sympathy for Fascism in another context (Cioran, 1995, 131).

aesthetically rooted in their own social context' (qtd in Bloch et al., 1980, 166). To that extent, their work remains unreconciled, critical of the social and political conditions from which it arises. As this Element will contest, the in some senses shared formal development in Beckett and Cioran after the Second World War is in itself constitutive of such a response. Therefore, it is both a stance derived from those times and a stance against their drift. In the process, Beckett and Cioran alter the relation between reading and writing, author and reader. In sometimes aggressive ways, both seek to confront and to undermine readerly expectations as a means to alter understandings with potential political, but certainly with critical and historical, implication.

This is all true of the moment in which Cioran and Beckett worked to produce kinds of writing new to them, a moment which establishes further significant parallels. *Précis de décomposition*, Cioran's first sustained text in French, was published at the end of September 1949; it was begun in 1946 (Cioran, 2011, 1315). Its publication occurred, in other words, towards the latter end of what commentators, echoing Beckett himself, have called 'the siege in the room', the concentrated production of those, then as yet largely unpublished, texts which he created between early 1946 and January 1950. Specifically the three novels *Molloy*, *Malone Dies*, and *The Unnamable* everywhere bear the marks, Andrew Gibson has argued, of the War and its aftermath of trial and trauma in France. They also defy, sometimes obliquely, sometimes more directly, the heroic and mythic narrative that Gaullist France deployed when seeking to heal (or at least to obscure the causes for) that trauma (Gibson, 2010, 115–16, 119–21). Cioran's *Précis de décomposition*, in a similarly oblique but resonant manner, spoke to the moment of its writing and publication. In an opening section, 'Généalogie du Fanatisme' [Genealogy of Fanaticsm] added late to his text, Cioran defended ideas which are in essence 'neutre' [neutral], against their being enacted in history, when they 'prend figure d'événement' [take on the aspect of an event]. Then are born 'les idéologies, les doctrines, et les farces sanglantes' [ideologies, doctrines, bloody farces] (Cioran, 2011, 1318, 3).

For Cioran, it is those who mobilise the idea in history *as* an event who are the truly guilty: 'Les vrais criminels sont ceux qui établissent une orthodoxie sur le plan religieux ou politique. [...] Lorsqu'on se refuse à admettre le caractère interchangeable des idées, le sang coule' [The real criminals are those who establish orthodoxy on religious or political grounds, who make distinction between the faithful and the schismatic. When one refuses to allow the inter-changeable character of ideas, blood flows] (Cioran, 2011, 4). Cioran's philo-sophical scepticism is grounded, then, in his attentiveness and eagerness to understand both the 'event' of the recent War and to recognise in it the inherent dangers of an aftermath in France where de Gaulle was potentially setting in train another bloody tragedy or farce.[12] In this, Cioran's stance might be said to echo Beckett's post-War positioning (Morin, 2017, 131). Whilst it might be impossible to refute Sontag's argument that, ultimately, Cioran (or Beckett) is trapped within his (or their) historical circumstance, therefore, it is also impossible to deny that both are attentive to and deeply anxious about their moment and situation – especially at the outset of their writing in a language relatively new to both in this regard, French.

It would also be true to say that both find the acuity of that attunement *in* the situation in which they found themselves, as both – for good or ill – adopted a particular role and character within this historical circumstance for particular reasons. For Beckett, who at this time was reaching a particular kind of impasse, at least in his prose writing, as we shall see, there are certainly conjunctions with Cioran's understanding of that circumstance and the perspective he establishes towards it.

For both Beckett and Cioran, finally, formal decisions are taken at this moment which, whilst they might not 'transvalue' 'historicizing consciousness', reveal the effects and marks of that consciousness, and, arguably, in their confrontational and intransigent demands, seek fully to address and understand it as a way of provoking change.

1.2 The Advantages of Exile – Beckett and Cioran in Paris

Cioran's early French writing maintains a radical stance towards his times and new context in his adopted city, Paris. In turn, some of the aspects of his stance parallel those which Beckett developed upon his return after the occupation of the city ended. This section will trace those aspects and begin to delineate strains and self-characterisations in Cioran's philosophy which in similar form also recast Beckett's writing from this point.

Précis de décomposition sees Cioran cast himself as an 'anti-philosophe' because of that historical situation. In order, as it were, to embody this stance, he then immediately adopts a self-characterisation which in itself also, however subliminally, revives something of the tensions of his pre-War politics. Cioran rapidly models what he calls the 'métèque' [immigrant/outsider] as an archetypically ideal modern persona. From *Précis* at the end of the 1940s through to the work of the 1970s, Cioran re-inflects this mask of the métèque, as we shall see, to make it into a more literary voice, or a voice outside history, until in the

---

[12] John Pilling, in an inaugural piece linking Beckett and Cioran, noted that it was only after the War that for both an 'essentially pessimistic vision' found 'a really individual medium', which involved switching to writing in French (Pilling, 1977, 306).

later work, as he confesses, the distance between the 'anti-philosophe' mask in this incarnation and his own face has narrowed to nothing.

Yet by the time Cioran first uses this characterisation in 1949, it is difficult to think he was unaware of the soiled and pejorative resonance the term had accrued in France. As Gérard Noiriel has established, across the 1920s and 1930s, the right-wing French press was deploying the term 'métèque' as meaning all foreigners who came to live in France, but particularly those like Cioran from Eastern Europe, who were seen as undermining native values and civilisation (Noiriel, 2007, 380). Both Noiriel and Michael Prazan point out the fact that within this blank prejudice against those who come from an unspecified 'Orient', it is especially Jewish people who are targeted. Prazan confirms that it was at this period that the label of 'Juif errant' [wandering Jew] assumed its full abhorrent currency, this figure being associated with the carrying of a sickness which will eventually infect the nation (Prazan, 2004, 76, 82, 91). Cioran's valorisation of the term 'métèque' is therefore typically and deliberately provocative; having lived in Paris in the later 1930s, he can hardly have been innocent of what he did when so embodying the persona. He is both dubiously taking the taint upon himself and presuming that it can deployed regardless of its racist resonance.[13]

Initially, at least, Cioran's characterisation seems to capture some of this human uncertainty and difficulty, one which displays a provocative but immature political understanding, in adopting the term 'métèque', and it is something of this human dilemma of the outsider or refugee which we will see also underlie Beckett's new formal and substantial work from *Textes pour rien* onwards. In a subsection of *Précis de décomposition*, 'Tribulations d'un métèque' [Trials of an Outsider], Cioran dramatises the implications of such a character: 'Amoureux de patries successives, il n'en espère plus aucune. [...] Citoyen du monde – et de nul monde – il est inefficace, sans nom et sans vigueur' [Loving countries in succession, he has no more hopes for any single one; [...] a citizen of the world, and of no world, he is useless, nameless, without energy] (Cioran, 2011, 97).[14] Strikingly, Cioran then voices some such métèque glossing his situation: 'Je me suis forgé d'innombrables idoles, ai dressé partout trop d'autels' [I've made numerous idols for myself, have set up too many altars all over the place]. Aimlessly seeking something to believe in

---

[13] Given Cioran's philosophical adherence to pre-Socratic Greek thinking, to be discussed later in this Element, his sense of the valorisation to be achieved through the 'métèque' idea to an extent embodies an equivocation around the ancient use of the term as meaning both 'a humiliated being' and also a 'privileged' free and self-made person, a worker essential to the proper functioning of ancient Athenian society (Whitehead, 1977, 1–2).

[14] Shane Weller has made play with the 'citizen of nowhere' trope as applicable to Beckett's later work particularly (Weller, 2021, 43).

some god, the émigré speaker is abandoned in a 'shroud of ennui'. As the momentum behind Cioran's perspective develops across *Précis*, this notion of the outcast lapsing into a version of decadence accumulates its furies – 'je ressens toute la pesanteur de l'espèce' [I resent all the burden of the species] (Cioran, 2011, 97–8).[15]

Cioran then casts this anger not through the voice of the anonymous métèque, but through the governing voice of his text, 'lorsqu'on revient à soi et que l'on est seul – *sans la compagnie des mots* – on redécouvre l'univers inqualifié, l'objet pur, l'événement nu' [when one returns upon the self and one is alone, *lacking the company of words*, one rediscovers the unqualified universe, the pure object, naked event] (Cioran, 2011, 115).[16] For Cioran, exile is from language as much as from nation state; exile enforces scepticism about all language, which might simply, after all, 's'envoler' [fly away].

Words are abstractions from realities; it is only when Adam was 'chased out of Paradise', Cioran avers, that he began baptising things with words, so setting in train the whole history of philosophy from Plato through Kant and Hegel.[17] By the end of the *Précis*, the métèque's situation has moved from a particular characterisation of an intimated slide towards decadence, to conceiving that situation as diagnostic of modernity: 'L'illusion moderne a plongé l'homme dans les syncopes du devenir, [. . .] il y a perdu [. . .] sa "substance"' [The modern illusion has cast humanity into the unconsciousness of becoming; [. . .] it has lost there [. . .] its "substance"] (116). The quotation marks around 'substance' in the original dramatize the distance from the real that Cioran's brief mapping of decomposition within history via the 'métèque' arrives at. As sustained later in Cioran's cited 1970 comparison of himself to Beckett around the 'impossibility of Being', humanity is suffering some kind of malady of perpetual process. 'Becoming' carried for Cioran none of its Heideggerian charge, but stood rather as a signature for the reversion which modern humans have suffered.[18] Cioran,

---

[15] John Pilling, in his advocacy for Cioran, goes so far as to argue that he 'is an addict of our decadence, so keen to see it continue, for if it is "encouraged" (and thereby "exhausted") it will allow "new forms" – hopefully the Void – into existence' (Pilling, 1979, 16).

[16] The end of the section about encountering suicide in Cioran's *Le mauvais démiurge* (1969) shows a similar movement in the text's speaker – 'For a long time, I built theories about man-outside-of-everything. Now I've become that man, I incarnate him' (Cioran, 2011, 671).

[17] This implication is charted copiously in Cioran's 1964 *La chute dans le temps* [*The Fall into Time*]. History erupts from that book's opening section 'L'Arbre de vie', which argues God's implication in Adam's Fall and the subsequent hounding of a humanity 'inadapté exténué et cependant indefatigable, sans racines' [exhausted yet tireless misfit without roots] (Cioran, 2011, 526).

[18] Cioran's *Cahiers* is notably dismissive of Heidegger's writing as just 'jargon', whilst at the same time crediting him, along with Céline, with being one of the few writers after Joyce to make language say something (Cioran, 1997, 673, 910). A similar uncertainty seems to underpin Cioran's responses through time to Maurice Blanchot, finding him one of the most 'profound'

in this regard, was acutely cognisant about that incapacity and limitation of which Sontag seemed to cast him as unaware; as moderns, for him, we each have lost our places and essence.

Obviously, as in some of Beckett's attitudes, such acuity of awareness depends upon experience. Cioran had spent three years as a student in Paris from 1937 before resuming his troubling connection with his home country, Romania, upon his return there in 1940. He delivered a radio address praising Corneliu Zelea Codreanu in the same year. Codreanu, who had recently been assassinated, was a charismatic leader of the nationalist and Fascist movement, the Iron Guard, in Romania. By the time of Cioran's return, Romania was under a military dictatorship led by Ion Antonescu; it was Antonescu who sent Cioran back to France as some kind of cultural attaché to the Vichy regime in 1941. After three months, however, Antonescu apparently fired Cioran from this post, although the reasons behind this, whether political, personal, or due to other misunderstandings, are not known. Ilinca Zarifopol-Johnston, whose *Searching for Cioran* provides a detailed account of Cioran's life in Romania and early years in Bucharest, Berlin and Paris, goes so far as describing the years 1937–45 as 'lost years' due to the scant documentary evidence available (Zarifopol-Johnston, 2009, 136–7). 'Lost' also in the sense too that, for Zarifopol-Johnston, Cioran's motivations in making the radio broadcast praising Codreanu are unknown, the reasons for his advocacy for certain Iron Guard doctrine are obscure, and his association with Antonescu is unexplained.[19] What is clear is that Cioran spent much time later disavowing these connections – although his preparation in 1991 of the new edition of *Romania's Transfiguration* of course only served to complicate all of these matters much further (176, 186).[20]

What is clear from the biography is that by 1943 Cioran was accepted amongst Latin Quarter intellectuals in Paris, and particularly amongst the group around Jean-Paul Sartre and Simone de Beauvoir. As Cioran was a regular attender at the Café de Flore during the latter phase of the Nazi occupation, his association with

---

writers of the time, yet also wilfully obscure and empty, meaningless, 'il n'ya que des mots', words, words, words (111, 544, 622). Cioran had publicly tangled with Blanchot in a series of articles written by each of them on the future of the novel in 1953 (Cioran, 2011, 1370).

[19] Cioran's status within Iron Guard circles has, however, been increasingly documented, as, for example, in Mircea Platon's citation of a letter from Codreanu to Cioran thanking him and praising him for writing *Romania's Transfiguration*. Broadly, Platon takes the scholarship as confirming that Cioran adopted a 'revolutionary', 'modernist' stance in his reading of the moment – one pro-European and indebted as so many were to the thinking of Oswald Spengler. Eclectically, this led to Cioran's admiration for Hitler, Mussolini, and Lenin (Platon, 2012, 65–6).

[20] Even privately, and as late as 1969, to himself in *Cahiers*, Cioran was dismissing his Iron Guard advocacy as 'une folie de jeunesse' [youthful madness], and resenting how this had prevented him espousing any further causes in others' eyes (Cioran, 1997, 708).

this group was clearly a factor in the immediate acclaim he received on the appearance of *Précis de décomposition* from Gallimard in 1949; the book was awarded the Rivarol Prize for the best work in French by a foreign author in 1950, and Cioran's reputation as a writer and philosopher was immediately guaranteed (this prevalence of praise for the work at its publication perhaps drew its attention to Beckett). The connection with the Café de Flore ambience was, however, impermanent. Cioran was shortly to distance himself from Sartre and he frequently disparaged Sartre's later writings.[21] He had also, early on, suffered disdain, which obviously rankled, from the French contemporary whose work might seem at that point most correlative to his own – Albert Camus (Zarifopol-Johnston, 2009, 5–7).

In post-War Paris, Cioran was joined by fellow Romanian émigrés who included Benjamin Fondane, the later playwright Eugène Ionesco, and the anthropologist Mircea Eliade. Cioran and Eliade particularly carried a burden of association with the Iron Guard through its key 'philosopher', the university professor and irrationalist philosopher Nae Ionescu. These self-exiles variously circled each other in the city from the later 1940s to the 1980s.[22] Cioran was the most decisive, however, in linking his decision to abandon the language of his early work in 1947 and write in French thereafter to an attempt to change his life and who he was. As he put it in interview, 'En changeant de langue, j'ai aussi liquidé le passé' [by changing the language I wrote in, I also liquidated my past] – a further provocation in the choice of verb. As he always told it, the 1947 switch of languages came to him when he was translating Mallarmé into Romanian in Dieppe and was suddenly struck by the absurdity of putting French into 'une langue que personne ne connaît' [a language no one understands]. Elsewhere in interviews, Cioran characterised the switch as a sudden suffering from 'le complexe du métèque' as an escapee from 'une province de Roumanie' who was drawn especially to Paris (Cioran, 1995, 22–3, 43–4). Romania, as he confirms always, was in his childhood a part of the Austro-Hungarian Empire, so Transylvania was to an extent a province of a colonised province.[23] Whilst there are obvious parallels here with Beckett's situation as an Irish writer

---

[21] *Cahiers* provides ample evidence of Cioran's excess and lack of self-attentiveness in some of those responses – Sartre's book on Genet of 1966, for instance, is called an event as monstrous as Auschwitz (Cioran, 1997, 413).

[22] Cioran's reminiscence of Eliade in 'Quelques Rencontres' typically does not mention the latter's politics, even when describing their meeting in Bucharest at the time Eliade was most involved with the Iron Guard (Cioran, 2011, 1202). Matei Calinescu has mapped the various associations and fallings out of this grouping in Paris and fully discussed the influence of Nae Ionescu (Calinescu, 2002, 657–64). Eugène Ionesco's 1959 play *Rhinoceros* was an attack on the adherents to Iron Guard ideology and on all believers in totalitarianism.

[23] Pascale Casanova takes Cioran's decision to relocate to France and adopt French as evidence that he figures amongst what she calls in her chapter title including him 'The Assimilated', as one of

settling in Paris (and, as we have seen, Cioran acknowledged Beckett's Irishness whilst also discounting it as not part of his modernity), Beckett's situation and adoption of French is obviously on very different grounds to Cioran's. His history in Paris, through the years at the École Normale and beyond, is wholly other.[24]

In Cioran's case, the immediate acceptance and praise for *Précis* must also be one factor behind the increasing confidence, and perhaps the increasing sense of being assimilated in the city and language, which underpins the immediate and important shift in focus around the topic of the métèque when Cioran returned to it in his next book, *La tentation d'exister* in 1956 – the immediate cause of Beckett's recommendation of Cioran's work in his correspondence of that and later years.[25] *Précis* had dramatised the métèque as a characteristic figure amidst a perceived increasing decadence of Western civilisation, culture, and philosophy – a figure, in fact, forced to become 'anti-philosophe'. By 1956, this characterisation has become slightly transposed, now as a specifically *literary* possibility, and therefore largely but qualifiedly one more full of promise than the dejected, uncertain, first figuration. *La tentation* measures the 'Avantages de L'Exil' specifically as the phenomenon is to be written out by novelists and poets. An exile is not someone who has 'abdiqué', given up; in fact, exiled writers are ambitious, 'agressif', and embittered. Nonetheless, as writers, exiles enjoy advantages over native authors.[26] They are challenged by the issue of whether they are able fully to adopt 'un autre idiome' [another idiom or style] and to renounce the language which encapsulates their past. 'Au certain point', 'il rompt' [they split], 'avec lui-même' [with themselves]. Yet, in this 1956 version of the argument, the exiled writer carries the 'advantage'; she or he has a story to tell to the modern world, a story of 'ses souffrances' [their sufferings]. The disadvantage is that the métèque's perspective becomes a kind of

---

the writers such as V. S. Naipaul and Cioran's friend Henri Michaux who, each coming from 'small countries', sought to succeed in a 'great literary Center' (Casanova, 2004, 215).

[24] Jean-Michel Rabaté has recently and persuasively linked Beckett's switch of languages to his historical and intertextual positioning with regard to Joyce, writer of all styles (2016, 133).

[25] In a telling parallel to the situation confronting Beckett by the end of the 1940s, the editorial material in Cioran's *Oeuvres* introducing *La tentation* notes that Cioran had come close to giving up writing by 1951; the bitterness of the self-critique in *Syllogismes de l'amertume*, following upon the self-diagnosis of *Précis*, brought Cioran 'à l'impasse'. The abundance of *La tentation*, which turned out as one of Cioran's longest texts, came only when he strove to turn the critique outwards, away from himself, and more towards 'la siècle'. Although *La tentation* deploys more expansive, essayistic, bursts of text, the manuscript shows they were often created through a 'collage' process of cutting up and assembling previous chunks of writing (Cioran, 2011, 1363, 1366).

[26] Zarifopol-Johnson has maintained that, for Cioran, unlike for postcolonial writers, exile and the 'self-renunciation' involved in it amounted to 'apotheosis of the creative self' (Zarifopol-Johnston, 2007, 31).

mannerism; their frequent and immediate success – such as that achieved by Cioran's own first book in Paris – traps them in a fate or repetition: 'on ne peut indéfiniment renouveler l'enfer' [you can't forever recycle Hell].

Ultimately, for Cioran, the exiled writer is a 'tragique' figure able to renew an adopted language through narrating their different experience, but never losing that sense of alienation, of loss of self, or of being able to imbue stories only with assimilated perspectives (Cioran, 2011, 302–3). Even in 1969 in *Cahiers* Cioran was meditating about 'le drame du métèque' as the drama of handling 'une langue qui n'est pas la sienne' [a language not their own].[27] The danger, again, is that writing in another language lapses into style, which is 'un mensonge', a lie (Cioran, 1997, 662). Those few able to achieve a 'triomphal' version of 'l'exil', in Cioran's view, such as the Guadeloupe-born Saint-John Perse, those able to replace 'le *Je*' by '*L'Étranger*', the 'I' by 'the stranger', were still those working in the official language of their birthplace (as Camus was also). They are able, despite their alienation, 's'accorder au monde' [to attune themselves to the world] (Cioran, 2011, 1197).

Frequently in his notebooks, Cioran adjures himself to 'continuer comme si rien n'était' [to carry on as though there were no issue], to 'travailler', work. He cannot overcome his story. He continues also to praise native writers such as the novelist Claude Simon, who have an advantage in being able to be 'présent dans chaque ligne', 'haletant' [present in every phrase, breathing] behind every adjective he creates (Cioran, 1997, 496). This general sense of incompatibility here, one which then resonates across Cioran's later career, had in fact already converged in the writing in the last few pages of *Précis*. The argument there praises those such as Kierkegaard and Nietzsche, who stand apart from their time, who are never not themselves, since the viscera and blood have made for their creation – 'l'on perçoit un *moi*' [there's a "I" to be seen] behind everything they write, and 'tout devient confession' [everything turns into confession with them] (Cioran, 2011, 160).[28]

---

[27] Cioran, like Beckett, spoke flawless French, but with a heavy accent which reportedly 'marked him as a foreigner' (Zarifopol-Johnston, 2009, xvi). Casanova has noted the typically antiquated and Racinian nature of Cioran's French written style, as though he sought to outdo the French themselves (Casanova, 2004, 216). André Bernold, whose memoir of Beckett quotes Cioran on him approvingly, has an interesting extension about Beckett as frequently finding himself a foreigner to himself: when thinking of his own earlier works, Beckett is reported several times to have said that 'he's become foreign to me, [...] I don't know this author' (Bernold, 2015, 65).

[28] In an interview, Cioran stated he saw all of his writing as autobiographical, and writing itself as a 'kind of necessity' which 'se vide', empties the 'moi' of the writer until 'il n'y a les restes d'eux-mêmes [...] c'est des fantoches' [they are only the remains of themselves, puppets] – Kleist again (Cioran, 1995, 304). Cioran felt that similar but positive voiding of the self came through adherence to Buddhism (82). Willis G. Regier has pointed to Cioran's lifelong admiration for Nietzsche's *Ecce Homo* as indicative of the displacement and connection Cioran perceived between a philosopher's life and writing (Regier, 2005, 84–5). John Pilling has

Yet, for Cioran, this cannot conceal the fact that minds matter only when they are at odds, and at odds with themselves. Being *'plusieurs'* several, sceptical and self-divided, they can never settle or choose to be themselves only (162). The penultimate page of *Précis* sees the 'moi' speaking through this text draw cause from such perception for self-loathing, 'et dans cette haine je rêve d'une autre vie, d'une autre mort' [in this hatred I dream of a different life, a different death] (161). In these late moments in the book, Cioran reprises his earlier section 'En l'Honneur de la Folie', with its quotation from Gloucester in *King Lear*, 'Better I were distract,' and makes a demented wish on behalf of the writing voice 'Vivre et mourir à la troisième personne' [to live and die in the third person], as though some displaced renderer of *Not I*, again (111).

Such wrestlings conjoin, of course, with much in Beckett's writing. If anything, though, Cioran's sense of his situation hardens in its irrevocability, as book after book followed *Précis*. Richard Howard's eloquent rendition of a passage from 1971's *Écartèlement* captures the resignation of all of this: 'Everything I have ventured, everything I have held forth on all my life is indissociable from what I have experienced. I have invented nothing. I have merely been the secretary of my sensations' (Cioran, 2012, 148).

What is notable about all of this writing as self-dictation, however, writing as direct expression of experience unmediated by an 'I', is that it hangs upon Cioran's thinking in this way through his attention to the situation of the métèque within modern actualities. The métèque, with all of its advantages, pleasures, sensations, loathings, rages, and aboulias. Cioran's sense of himself as an observer of the immediate post-War culture and society of France exacerbates his scorn for its failings, but also enhances the 'sensation' of his own severalness and unsettledness, his writing as a *'moi'* in the wake of Kierkegaard and Nietzsche, but attuned to his place late in history. As 'L'Homme Vermoulou', Worm-Eaten Humankind – the last section of the opening title page of *Précis* – sees it, 'je ne dirai plus "Je suis"' [I'll never again say "I am"], since 'Ce temps est révolu où l'homme se pensait en termes d'aurore' [the time is gone when humans thought of themselves as a dawn] (Cioran, 2011, 90).[29]

Much of this thinking through of the métèque's unique but representative stance is consonant with the version of Beckett found in Cioran's more ephemeral commentaries upon his 'bon ami'. From the mid-1980s onwards, Cioran

---

noted that this aspect of Cioran's thinking was demonstrated too by his predilection for 'the great unclassifiable writers of diaries and letters and aphorisms' as his favoured reading matter (Pilling, 1979, 15).

[29] *The Unnamable*'s re-expressing himself as 'Worm' in the novel Beckett was creating from March 1949 is not remote from Cioran's perception of a post-War humanity reduced to its least hopeful aspects (Beckett, 2010b, 51).

was asked relatively frequently in interviews about his friendship, which was clearly by then widely known about; Cioran developed decisive lines in response, perhaps through the very repetition of such questions. Although he has been in Paris for many years, Cioran avers, Beckett has not been acclimatised to French intellectual life; 'il est resté un étranger' [he remained a stranger] (Cioran, 1995, 210). Shortly after Beckett's death, Cioran recounted that Beckett had supported him financially with some of his Nobel Prize money and that the French had always misunderstood Beckett. Beckett always seemed in fact to have showed up in Paris as if only yesterday, fallen from the moon, despite his long residence: Beckett's failure to be tainted by his surroundings was 'ahurissant' [astounding] (235–6). Beckett's conversation was not at all interesting, but there was something profound about him (270). This might be, perhaps, because Beckett was an extremely lucid man, 'qui ne réagit pas en écrivain' [he never responded to anything as a writer would]. 'Il a un style de vie à lui, c'est un cas tout à fait à part' [He had a style of life all his own, his is a case totally apart] (304–5). The awkward, ill-adapted but composed implication of all of this resonates with Beckett's own writing of this period, as he sought new forms through breaking from the old in the years after the War.

1.3 Beckett and the métèque in *Textes pour rien/Texts for Nothing*

Beckett's prose writing from the year and more just after Cioran's *Précis de décomposition* seems fraught and freighted with similar intractibilities to those found there, and then revisited and reinvigorated across Cioran's career. In the end, these intractibilities involve the formal decision that Beckett's previously elaborate, sustained prose texts must give way to short, often inconclusive units and shapes. These shapes in their turn express the syntactic and consonant uncertainty around identity and knowledge that characterise the mid-late Beckett prose.

The resigned vow of continuation amidst exhaustion at the end of *The Unnamable* brought to an ambiguous stop the voicings through character of that and the previous novels, *Molloy* and *Malone Dies*. *Texts for Nothing*, written in French between late 1950 and late 1951, notably begins in continuation, but through reversal of that vow: 'Suddenly, no, at last, long last, I couldn't any more, I couldn't go on' (Beckett, 2010a, 3). 'Continuer' is the French verb Beckett translated as 'go on' – his translation from the original French *Textes*. This translation was begun in 1951 but completed only in December 1966 (Beckett, 1958, x, 115). But this voice of the first *Text* is no longer an 'I' however dubiously graced by a name; in fact, this 'I' knows the names of his predecessors Molloy and Malone. He asks a shrewd question about a Pozzo whilst also averring in line with his immediate predecessor that 'nothing is namable' (Beckett, 2010a, 18, 21, 45). Despite such familiarity, in other words, the 'I' of *Texts for Nothing*, for the first time in Beckett's work, carries no clear named identity himself – he has escaped the fate even of Cioran's Adam.[30] Whatever else he is, though, he is a métèque in similar ways to the figure so characterised by Cioran – someone who has, by continuing, moved away, including away from himself, by the end of the *Texts*. He has become a dweller in 'les patries successives', but also through successive and contradictory versions of himself.

Strikingly, and perhaps because of the protracted excruciation of the translation process, the differences between Beckett's original French and the English version, *Texts for Nothing*, flitter around variant dilemmas and helplessness for their anonymous métèque protagonist. This is the extrapolation on the opening page of the first of the *Texts*, which reports injunctions from others that the speaker stay where he is – but he cannot stay 'Home' or return to it. Notably, in the English, that 'home' is initially called a 'den', predicting the scene of Beckett's later drama *Krapp's Last Tape* (1958) and emphasising the speaker's creatureliness.[31] Instead of 'den', the French text has the more neutral 'coin', anything from a simple 'place' or 'spot' to any street corner (Beckett, 2010a, 3; 1958, 116).[32]

The theme is taken up decisively at the opening of the second Text, where the speaker bizarrely finds himself under a 'glass', or 'cloche' in French, as though a stuffed animal, but notes that this is 'not long habitable either,' or rather 'vite inhabitable'. The interesting switch between the negative French and the qualified English continues as the speaker moves to generalisation – 'where you are will never long be habitable', or 'partout où l'on sera ce sera inhabitable' (Beckett, 2010a, 7; 1958, 123). The English allows for at least some time for habitation compared to the more adamant truth of the speaker's permanently unhoused situation in French.

By the end of Text II, the speaker has no sense of to what it is they may return; yet, by the later pages of Text III, to prevent himself breaking out into tears, this speaker conjures a crony for company, a 'fellow warrior', one from the navy in

---

[30] Zarifopol-Johnston points out that Cioran's name went through various alterations and that the final version is in fact partly 'made up', deploying the initials of an unlikely source of which Cioran had become aware – the English writer E. M. Forster. There was no unlikelier or alien source than that (Zarifopol-Johnston, 2009, 8).

[31] Jonathan Boulter has measured Beckett's use of 'den' here against Heidegger's concept of 'thrownness' (Boulter, 2019, 200).

[32] In a statement that will prove proleptic for this study of the correspondences between Beckett and Cioran, the protagonist of *The Calmative* (1946) says that he has moved his 'refuge' so often, he can no longer 'tell between dens and ruins' (Beckett, 2009c, 19).

the First World War under Admiral Jellicoe – but also someone in the French from 'ma promotion, un pays', 'my own vintage, my own bog'. Amidst this strange jarring historicisation, which establishes a shadow from the First World War across the century as backdrop to the speaker's current situation, the Text includes another call – 'We have well deserved our motherland', or 'Nous avons bien mérité de la patrie', this last a phrase with ambiguous resonance in Gaullist France (Beckett, 2010a, 13; 1958, 133). That patriotic call from the natal country for which he is fit, however, will, for both the crony and the speaker, lead only to the hospital (in the French), or the Incurables (English) – the designation of those so damaged, either by shell shock or by their wounds, in the First World War for whom there was perceived to be no hope (Davies, 2020, 210).[33]

By the opening of Text IV, 'il rompt avec lui-même', in Cioran's terms, the speaker is clearly self-divided. Seeking a 'simple' answer to the question 'who says this [...]?' the text becomes tortuous – and the French is more expressive in making this into a question in this instance, 'qui parle ainsi, se disant moi' [who speaks in this way, speaking itself 'me'?]. The French answer to the question is initially more straightforward than Beckett's later translation – it's 'la même inconnu que toujours' [the same unknown presence as usual].[34] But then it veers into further complication – the same one for whom I always exist, in the hollows of my inexistence, 'de la sienne, de la nôtre' – both *its* inexistence, *and* all of ours? 'Here's a simple answer', the end of the original French sentence mischievously avers. It is unclear where the 'ours' derives from the 'its' or 'his', beyond the suggestion of common plight (Beckett, 1958, 139).[35] Beckett's Englishing of the answer to the question here of who speaks is as strained, but also notable in designating the condition of the speaker: 'It's the same old stranger as ever, for whom alone accusative I exist' (Beckett, 2010a, 17). Beckett's weird intonation loses the commonality of the French around this condition and renders it all in that self-alienated state concomitant to Rimbaud's 'Je est un autre'. 'Accusative' asserts the 'you' within the 'I', but also acts as a kind of participle, the 'I' accusing the lonely stranger for its lack of connections.

---

[33] The speaker continues in this vein with a bizarre smack at the transnational story of the British royal family, the Windsors, or Hanovers, or even the Hohenzollerns is it? (Beckett, 2010a, 13).

[34] Cioran's sense that native writers such as Claude Simon are everywhere present as themselves in their texts comes to mind in counterposing this notion of a writer/speaker 'inconnu' 'toujours' [always unknown], to itself in a text.

[35] Jonathan Boulter has pointed to the implications of Beckett's use of language in *Texts* around subjectivity – 'that which confines and configures the subjectivity of the subject [...] is also that which by definition as waste, must be cast out. [...] Narrative becomes what Georges Bataille calls the "accursed share, the excess which defines the subject"' (Boulter, 2002, 3).

The 'inconnu' has also achieved firm and contemporary status, in Beckett's translation, as 'the same old stranger' – Camus's 1942 novella having received Beckett's prior acknowledgement in a letter ('important') (Beckett, 2011, 32).[36]

Such splittings accumulate across *Texts for Nothing* until by the end of the penultimate piece, XII, we move towards a decisive sense of the relation between a divided and discontinuous self and its social or existential situation. This time, the French feels more judicious in diagnosing the situation: 'que dire de cet autre, qui divague ainsi, à coups de moi à pourvoir et de lui dépourvus, cet autre sans nombre ni personne dont nous hantons l'être abandonné, rien' (Beckett, 1958, 199).[37]

This ricochets between subject positions, moi/lui/nous, all of which ghost the others, before landing on the 'nothing' to say or be said. The inversion of the syntax ironically allows for the accumulation of possible identities and (dis-)empowerments before stealing all away. In his English version, Beckett goes fully métèque in rendering this complex and self-defeated exasperation: this 'other' notably becomes merely the 'latest' other amidst 'his babble of homeless mes and untenanted hims' (Beckett, 2010a, 50). Babbling as Babel-ing in this unfixed and unmoored world. ('Homeless mes' even has the look of English/French, homeless 'mys'). Where the French version of this sentence originally had suggested some possibility of happening, 'pouvoir', the English establishes an absolute condition of wandering incoherence, the 'pell-mell babel' of words and silences we hear about at the end of Text VI (27). The 'untenanted' situation of everything by the end of Text XII, however, comes back to a full stop with the sense that it all leads to similarly paronomasiac 'mots morts', nothing ever but dead words (50).

These switchings back and forth around enablement and disablement between, for Beckett, the original second-language French text and the first-language English text, are intriguing when read alongside Cioran's argument that this is our modern situation and consciousness. The English resonates more fully with a sense of 'home' and the consequent now, the crisis of homelessness, through wishing to 'dwell', for however short a time. The English has a lingering sense of the 'habitable' when the French merely avers that

---

[36] John Pilling noted that the parallels between Beckett and Cioran were striking in Text IV – for both writers, fiction itself clearly provided freedom and what Pilling calls 'refuge' – and Pilling sees this Beckett work as coming closest in tone to Cioran's discussion of these issues in *Précis* (Pilling, 1977, 309).

[37] Literally, in my translation, 'What to say about this other, who rambles on, enablingly so for me, disenablingly for him, this other without number or person whose deserted being we haunt, nothing.'

everything is 'inhabitable' and always will be.[38] It is as though the language Beckett was hearing around him every day in post-War Paris confirmed his bereftness: English, 'motherland', French 'la patrie'; Irish-English, 'bog', French 'un pays'.

This sense of the particular in location, amidst a general sense of dislocation, underlies further aspects of the *Texts*, more literal ones. 'It's not me, it can't be me', the speaker frets in VIII, wondering where it was exactly he lost his head or left it behind. By this point, he has become a ventriloquist's dummy, uttering that he must have left his head 'in Ireland, in a saloon'. But now where is he? 'To my certain knowledge ... somewhere in Europe probably' – the English version heightens the joke as the French text has no equivalent for 'certain' in 'certain knowledge' (34–5). But this is a voice who also knows the obscure Glasshouse Street, which is not far from the also-mentioned Piccadilly Circus in London; the Place de la République in Paris, associated oddly here with a memory of a blind man with an ear trumpet (so doubly exiled from the world), and the physical aspects of a pissoir on the corner of the Rue d'Assas (25, 35, 46). This is a speaker, then, at least familiar with major spaces, but also less-known places and utilities, in several cities, and 'probably' still somewhere amongst them.

Thinking in the wake of Cioran's characterisation of similar figures in *Précis*, from his similar experience of being in Paris both in the War and its aftermath, it would be difficult not to read something of the mobile trans-European biography of the speaker into the hesitations which in turn characterise the *Texts*. The first Text has a moment of unravelling around precisely the 'certain'. Thinking about moving on, he muses:

> One thing at least is certain, in an hour it will be too late, in half-an-hour it will be night, and yet it's not, not certain, what is not certain, absolutely certain, that night prevents what day permits (5).

The original French conveys the syntactic indirection of this more forcefully by building in an extra clause – 'ce n'est pas sûr, quoi donc, qu'est-ce que n'est pas sûr, absolument sûr' (Beckett, 1958, 119). The speaker twice asks himself what it is that is not certain about the esoterically worded difference between day and night, where the English is the more adamant about uncertainty itself, 'not, not'. Dubiety about location elsewhere in *Texts* is mirrored, then, into the broader epistemological questions which underwrite them.

---

[38] This tension is evident still in the repeated, almost ironic mannerism which spans two late Beckett texts. *Company* reflects on distance travelled across a life, without ever really proceeding in other senses far from 'home. Home!' The same reflex occurs twice in *Ill Seen Ill Said*, although there is also a consolatory sigh: 'Home at last' (Beckett, 2009a, 40, 56, 64, 62).

These are no longer the comical and exhausting workings through in the terms of *Watt*, where all possibilities of understanding and misunderstanding are given vent and event. Nor are they the contrasts evident in *Murphy*, whose eponymous émigré's Odyssean wanderings 'to find home' are replaced by Celia's new certainty after his obliteration, as she pushes Mr Kelly up a hill in the novel's last paragraph, since 'there was no shorter way home' (Beckett, 2009b, 4, 175). More, the syntactic indirections and compactings in both versions of *Textes/Texts* convey a synthesised embodiment of the experience and feeling of uncertainty itself, its self-misdirections, even self-cancellings. The end of Text V sees the speaker's self-interrogation placing him in a kind of dock at a trial ('accusative'), haunted by 'phantoms' who 'speak his name', as though rarely establishing who he is. But the passage closes with a question about whether the 'name' will register when spoken to 'others, who will not believe them either, or who will believe them too' (Beckett, 2010a, 23). This complicates the relation between 'either' and 'too', as though it was possible to link the notion of a myriad of 'other' incomprehenders to some supplementary way of believing in his name. The French original says it all more directly and absolutely, here, 'qui ne les croiront pas, ou qui les croiront' (Beckett, 1958, 150–1). Either you believe or you do not believe, no either *and* too.

What is notable across the *Texts* is the speaker's seeming ease when such uncertainty of address or understanding happens within the felt presence of place. This punctures through suddenly at the end of Text III, after a passage where the speaker mulls literally discomposing himself by shedding a limb or two and existing just as a head, before reckoning on the losses of so doing. But such potential dis-composition is transposed immediately into an urge to set out on a spring morning of sun and rain 'from Duggan's door' 'not knowing if you'll ever get to evening, what's wrong with that? It would be so easy' (Beckett, 2010a, 14). The French has 'l'incertitude de pouvoir aller jusqu'au soir', a nicer sense of uncertainty once again, but now potentially including continuation or not as movement, as opposed to the restricted English temporal implication (Beckett, 1958, 136). The 'not I' is present here, 'still not me' in English, 'n'est toujours pas moi' in French, 'not always me' – an interesting split once more between a potential arrival at a self as opposed to a sense of discontinuity within the self. (That sense of discontinuity surely also has much to do with the considerably more 'alien' occurrence of 'Duggan's' in the French text – Beckett's translation finds *some* equivalents for locales in French, but notably not in all cases, as here.) The English 'moi' still might arrive somewhere, or home.

But, in both versions, the moment of setting out from Duggan's conveys also a moment of living with uncertainty, as does the heady ease at the end of Text VII, set in the Third Class waiting room of the South-Eastern Railway

Terminus, or 'la gare du Sud-Est'. From there, it is possible to have a sense of a full day 'pour me tromper, pour me ratrapper, pour me calmer, pour renoncer' [to go wrong, to catch myself up, to relax, to disavow] (Beckett, 1958, 164). The English version is much more complacent and unadventurous about the day's potentialities – 'to go wrong, to go right, to calm down, to give up' (Beckett, 2010a, 30). Both versions are in agreement, though, that there is nothing to fear because the ticket the speaker holds is valid for life(!).

Of course such moments of acceptance of uncertainty, or care-lessness, are rare and brief, even within the brief *Texts for Nothing*. The speaker in this one at the Terminus chides himself for his mistake; cities are not 'eternal' and there-fore neither are moments within them, however lived to the full. Text VII ends with a fraught sense of time passing and of the literal physical destruction wrought upon those former places both of possibility and of a kind of fulfilment. The French text imagines the station now 'à l'abandon', 'abandoned', and the glass of the waiting-room door 'd'une poussière de ruine', 'a dust of ruins'; the English drives the point home through repetition, the station 'in ruins,' and the door glass 'black with the dust of ruins' (Beckett, 2010a, 31). As a place, it cannot literally or through memory be returned to, and the final sentence of VII sees the speaker having to end by beginning again.[39]

It is important that the lack of sureness here seems to depend upon the notion that the *place* will have disappeared. (Interestingly, the Harcourt Street Terminus in Dublin did not close until December 1958, making the French Text VII prophetic, and the English, published in 1967, a *fait accompli*.) The memory and its potential is futile for this speaker in face of the inexistence of the place in which it was established, making the 'untenanted' nature of the speaker's current situation all the more confirmed. As with Cioran's sense of the métèque, this speaker is cast in a zone of the 'intemporel', 'inefficace, sans nom et sans vigueur', 'not in time', 'useless, nameless, without energy'. He cannot move on. Like Cioran's figuring of Adam, he is plagued by 'les syncopes de devenir' [unconsciouness of becoming], continually exiled from any sense of settledness and certainty, of being rather than becoming.

In *La tentation d'exister*, Cioran has a suggestive riff on the attractions of the French language for a non-native writer. 'L'étranger débridé', the 'fetterless stranger', Cioran argues, is 'amoureux d'improvisation et de désordre', 'loves improvisation and disorder'. By working in French, 'il se guérit de son passé, [. . .] se simplifie, devient *autre*' [heals himself of his past life, [. . .] simplifies himself, becomes *someone else*] (Cioran, 2011, 347). But this does not in itself

---

[39] Boulter illustrates this 'doubt' about an ability to pass from past to present in this moment in the 'Text' through Katherine Hayes's concept of 'distributed cognition' (Boulter, 2019, 233).

mean that the French language forms a haven; the French love of words is now a vice, at the expense of 'des choses', the very 'things' the words try to talk about. French, according to Cioran, is characterised by scepticism about everything, but particularly attuned 'de *formuler* nos doutes', a propensity to allow us 'to formulate or define those doubts'. In every sensitive civilisation, there now works 'une disjunction radicale entre la réalité et le verbe' [a rooted disjunction been reality and language] (350–1).

Comparison of Beckett's original French *Textes pour rien* with its English version, fifteen years in the making, shows him adopting an interesting practice between the orderly and the disorderly around such concerns; at moments in the English, the nostalgic pull seems stronger than in the more neutral or simple either/or French version of 'nos doutes'. The sense of the 'ruins' to which all of this, past and present, must come is concomitantly the more forceful in the English texts.[40] And yet with the French version that sense of living with 'l'incertitude' perhaps feels more distinct, alienated, less qualified by glimpses of possibility, certitude, or even rest. As a post-War writing, *Textes pour rien* offers a sense that a new start must be made beyond the frenzied but sustained textual outpourings from 'the siege in the room'; it offers a more conditioned sense of the travails of the 'I' than the recently finished and expansive three novels *Molloy, Malone Dies*, and *The Unnamable*. Beckett's concentrated prose and syntactical misdirections and delays in *Textes* integrate that precise scepticism which Cioran, also around these years, found in the French language, 'sceptique de nos possibilités' [sceptical of our possibilities]. Formally, that scepticism is reflected in the brevity of the Texts, the way they themselves break off to restart on different terms, sustainability breaking as the post-War world evolves its own increasing uncertainty and misdirection.[41]

In his very useful summary of Beckett's interests, involvements, and connections in 'Post–World War Two Paris', Shane Weller has demonstrated that 'his oeuvre shares [. . .] a number of major preoccupations' with thinkers such as Sartre, Camus, and those in the circles of art, philosophy, and what we would now call modernist publication. Whilst entering proper caveats about the limits to which 'context' can ever influence artistic form, Weller also establishes that the

---

[40] Beckett's alertness to the word in the English tradition stayed with him from early to late. Pope's *Essay on Man*, subject of his study at TCD, according to Frederik N. Smith, is quoted in the 'Sottisier' Notebook in the late 1970s: 'Who sees with equal eye, as God of all, | A zero perish or a sparrow fall, | Atoms of systems into ruin hurled, | And now a bubble burst, and now a world' (Smith, 2002, 12; Beckett, UoR MS 2901, 2r).

[41] Emilie Morin does not consider *Texts for Nothing*, but her chapter 3 on the 'Aftermath' of the War and what she calls the 'shift' in Beckett's work that took place from writing deploying 'the material of experience' to that of the 'material of expression' provides eloquent background to the historical and political situation in France at this point (Morin, 2017, 130–83 at 183).

cultural background of Paris, and figures including Bataille, Blanchot, and Robbe-Grillet, were vital to establishing the significance of Beckett's writing within his immediate situation. They aided the perception of him as a major writer in France before his reputation in the anglophone world was equally established (Weller, 2013, 164–5, 170). Cioran is absent from Weller's survey, but it is clear that he also shares with Beckett some affinity, perhaps a closer one than those in Weller's native list. Cioran is a 'métèque' also writing his first extended works in French at a point when Beckett is working through his 'siege'. Then, in 1950, the year after the publication of *Précis de décomposition*, Cioran also confronts the need to work in new forms, having as it were worked through his revisions of all the old ones. Whilst it is probably not possible definitively to establish when Beckett first read *Précis*, other than to know that it was at some point between 1949 and 1956, there are definite formal conjunctions and affinities between aspects of the 'new' Beckett writing and Cioran's 'take' upon the moment in which the two, although not knowing each other personally yet, were situated.

For both Beckett and Cioran, as they moved deeper into the 1950s and the nightmares in France continued, it is clear that correlative and escalated disillusion exacerbated the 'décomposition' to which their texts are subjected. In this disillusion, evidenced as formal brevity and inconclusion, lies their response to that 'historicized consciousness' of Sontag or the manifestation of an Adorno-style politics. 'Les creations de l'esprit' [inspired creations] 'suivent le destin de nos humeurs, de notre âge, de nos fièvres, et de nos déceptions' [follow the fated pathway of our moods, of our times, our passions and their disappointments], as Cioran concludes (Cioran, 2011, 135).[42] Beckett's efforts in a new form with *Textes pour rien*, and then in 'From an Abandoned Work', written in English in 1954, show him adopting a first-person anonymous persona whose thought meanders where it will, yet in more intense and concentrated ways even than in the preceding longer fictions. These latter texts are less formulated, more phases ready to break off once, as it were, the particular moment, mood, humour, or spasm has passed.

'From an Abandoned Work', when published in the mid-1950s, after all even 'advertised' its' being 'à l'abandon', as it were, like the imagined Sud-Est Railway Terminus. The narrator of this English text describes himself on its first page as 'Feeling awful, very violent', as though hungover with recent historical event and lashing out.[43] Such clouding is heard in Cioran too – immediately after those

---

[42] In interviews, Cioran noted that it was not that the ideas he has spawned the writing, but the other way about, that the mood dictated the writing, which then arrived at the idea (Cioran, 1995, 151).

[43] Beckett's work of the 1960s too seems to teeter on this cusp, even within the hermetically sealed cylinder of *The Lost Ones* (1970). This account notes many 'scenes of violence' between the bodies and wonders whether the place is 'doomed' to a future of anarchy, fury, and violence (Beckett, 2010a, 117, 119). It is as though the fanatical control of and in some of these mid-period Beckett works is balanced against a Yeatsian sensibility and reaction towards modern futility.

phrases just quoted about inspiration, he writes that 'Nous mettons en question tout ce que nous aimions autrefois [...] car tous est valuable – et tout n'a aucune importance' [we put into question what we formerly loved [...] for everything has value, everything is redundant].

That sense of lostness and not-knowing, however, seems more than adequate. In interviews, Cioran sees himself as operating between two modes of writing, the one 'violent, explosive', the other sardonic, 'cold'. The writing veers between the aggressive and the indifferent, and in this seems to strike accord (Cioran, 1995, 46, 61). Zarifopol-Johnston quotes a celebratory review of *Précis* by Maurice Nadeau on its publication, greeting the 'arrival' of 'the prophet of our era of concentration camps and collective suicide'. The book's advent 'has been prepared by all the philosophers of the void and of the absurd'.[44] Nadeau's response leaves no doubt as to the historical importance perceived in Cioran's book as witness to 'our times', times to which, as we have seen, the book only ever obliquely refers (Zarifopol-Johnston, 2009, 5). The sense of a look backwards and a look ahead is prevalent in Beckett's work too at this moment – and had been laid grounds for in this sense by the conjunction between his early interests within philosophy, and those which 'prepared' Cioran for the writing of *Précis de décomposition*.

2 Not Forgiving Life – Pessimism and Scepticism

2.1 'The Felt Need for Redemption'

Cioran's philosophy, or 'anti-philosophie', established parameters and diagnoses which sit in their ramifications alongside some of Beckett's familiar characterisations and imagery. In turn, those parameters issue in a similar and ever-more-pressing call for new formal exploration. This section will therefore lay out in more detail the origins and prompts behind Cioran's scepticism before suggesting those strains in Beckett's understanding of the history of Western philosophy which signal 'fraternal' understanding with something of Cioran's position.

'Si la philosophie n'avait fait aucune progrès depuis les pré-socratiques, il n'y aurait aucune raison de s'en plaindre' [If philosophy had made no progress since the Presocratics, there would be no reason to complain about that], Cioran contests in a subsection of *Précis de décomposition* calling for a 'Retour aux Éléments' (Cioran, 2011, 49). Although he completed his undergraduate thesis on the intuitionism of Henri Bergson and read extensively as a postgraduate in

---

[44] Nadeau much later reminisced, though, that on reading *Molloy* he had felt that Beckett had already gone further than those 'tenants de "l'absurde"', Cioran and Ionesco (Nadeau, 1990, 364).

Nietzsche, Georges Simmel, and Schopenhauer, Cioran's philosophical writing is always about a desired return to origins. Those origins are, consistently for him, evident amongst early Greek philosophy's attempts to understand 'the elements' out of which they felt the world and existence to be constituted (Zarifopol-Johnston, 2009, 71, 81–3).

Indeed, philosophy's movement away from these early concepts is cast by Cioran once again as a kind of expulsion-from-Eden moment when 'nous avons perdu [...] la comprehension du Destin' [we lost touch with our understanding of our destiny]. The history of philosophy for Cioran is one in which over-complication and indefinite usages of self-generating professional jargon persistently but increasingly obscure the truths which the discipline claims to reveal. In 1968, we find him mulling the 'prolixity' of German philosophers and poets in his *Cahiers*: the work of Hegel, Schopenhauer, 'even' Nietzsche, would be much better if it were cut to half the length, he contends. Consequently, 'on devrait philosopher comme si la "philosophe" n'existait pas' [One should do philosophy as if "philosophy" didn't exist at all] (Cioran, 1997, 581). Given the other parts of *Précis* that see the 'métèque' as the typical modern figure, it is once more difficult not to read such sentiments against history and professional 'progress' in similar vein.

And of course 'philosophy' does exist, and Cioran's writings make complex engagement and negotiation with it. This is so, however uncomfortable he might have been, and however he felt the need to correct anyone who called him a 'philosopher', because 'He was not interested in "objective" truth, and was bored with the need to argue and demonstrate' (Zarifopol-Johnston, 2009, 71–2).[45] Cioran's account, then, continues that early sense of history in philosophy as a fall away from its Presocratic in-placeness and essence. To this extent, Cioran's thinking sustains something of a Bergsonian intuitionism – 'Tout ce qui respire se nourrit d'invérifiable; un supplément de logique serait funeste à l'existence' [everything that breathes feeds upon the unverifiable; an addition of logic would desolate existence], as an early section in *Précis*, titled 'Variations sur la Mort', has it (Cioran, 2011, 10). Cioran repeatedly casts the application of any aspect of philosophical logic as fatal.[46] But then so are any

---

[45] Sylvain David has constructed a trajectory for Cioran's career around this issue, and weighed its formal implications in Cioran's work. Having set out with an aphoristic approach to the 'moi' and interiority, David sees the works of the 1960s beginning with *Histoire et utopie* as an attempt to treat of larger eternal 'themes' through more sustained essayistic works by Cioran. The 'third phase' then sees him 'passé à une reflexion d'avantage personelle, ancrée dans son experience propre' [passed on to reflection of personal benefit, fixed in his own experience] – but without the oscillations and self-divisions of *Précis* and the other early texts (David, 2006, 117–18, 218).

[46] Calinescu points to the sustained 'irrationalist' influence of his professor Ionsecu in Cioran's later thinking; Zarifopol-Johnston references a note to himself without a date in which Cioran, seemingly defending *Romania's Transfiguration*, suggests the continuing influence for him of

applications of the traditional terms and languages of philosophy. This is the result of the 'décomposition' and decadence in which history finds itself – 'la misère de *l'expression*, [. . .] l'indigence des mots dans leur épuisement et leur degradation' [poverty of *expression*, [. . .] hollowness of words in their exhaustion and degraded state] (Cioran, 2011, 20).

Out of this historical understanding arises in Cioran a defence of scepticism – 'N'y échappent que les sceptiques (ou les néants et les estètes)' [only the sceptics, nonentities and aesthetes escape] from the rampant fanaticism of recent history we hear on the second page of *Précis* (4). Later, the ancient sceptics and the French moralists are linked as those few who do not seek to apply ideas in a dangerous attempt 'modèler l'homme' [to shape other humans] (25). It is only these sceptics and moralists, in other words, who leave their readers free, whilst pointing to the errors in all systems. As the inclusion of the 'néants' in the list just provided perhaps indicates, Cioran's thinking is drawn to those who have no designs, in fact to those who withdraw from the normal functioning of system. In a contention that would have cheered Murphy himself, 'les désoeuvrés [. . .] sont plus profonds que les affaires. [. . .] La paresse est un scepticism physiologique' [the non-workers [. . .] see more deeply into things than men of business. Laziness is bodily scepticism] (23). Towards the end of *Précis*, Cioran asserts that 'L'Histoire confirme le scepticism' [history proves the truth of scepticism]; however 'elle n'*est* et ne *vit* qu'en le piétant' [it can only *be* or *live* by being trampled all over] (157). It is notable, again, that Cioran casts what thrives as that which is considered unacceptable and that which attracts hostility.

To confirm the 'truth' of scepticism is by default to both attract and to demonstrate antagonism to and difference from all other orders and sets of ideas. This pitches Cioran's writings interestingly; they take on something of the bitter impatience of Nietzsche, wrecking sacred ideals, but do not seek to propose any alternative version of life. They remain ultimately within a satiric mode. Each subsection of Cioran's books, whether longer and more like a developed essay, or more fragmentary, or simply aphoristic, seeks to discover a language which might approximate more closely to reality than philosophical tradition, in his view, allows.[47] Yet at the same time, and as with Beckett, each book is pitched against the drift of the times whilst constantly finding new ground for itself and a new mode in doing so. The origins of this in Beckett's understanding of the history of philosophy offer correlatives and divergences which we will now move on to.

---

anti-rationalist right-wing and anti-Semitic figures, including Maurice Blanchot, Benjamin Fondane, and Otto Weininger (Calinescu, 2002, 655; Zarifopol-Johnston, 2009, 115–17) .

[47] Florin Oprescu notes that the filiation between the fragmentariness of Cioran's *Cahiers* and that in his philosophical publications amounts to an 'organic epistemology', an 'exercise in authenticity' that runs across genres (Oprescu, 2013, 183).

What is intriguing at this point, where an inverted theology seems to meet with a sceptical, even pessimistic philosophical world view through history, is to see how Beckett's experience of philosophy before the Second World War prepared him for that sense of recognition that clearly came to him upon reading Cioran at some point in the late 1940s or early 1950s. This experience prepared also Beckett's at least partial, or largely partial, enthusiasm for many aspects of Cioran's writing, often out of his shared interest in particular philosophers, including the early Greeks. As Peter Fifield and others have noted, Beckett was deeply fascinated by the Presocratic philosophers. In the '*Philosophy Notes*', which Beckett gathered for himself in the 1930s, are extensive sections relating to all of the major figures from this first period of philosophy (Feldman and Mamdani, 2015, 135–42). But this kind of shared emphasis extends not only to Beckett's attention to the *kinds* of philosophy promoted by Cioran, but also to the choices made *within* and towards the history of philosophy itself.

Beckett's '*Philosophy Notes*' show him cognisant, or at least prompt him to be cognisant, about the origins of pessimism and scepticism, along with Stoicism and Epicureanism, in the work of the ancient Sophists (450– 400 BC) and the Hedonists (Beckett, 2020, 181). It is the Sophists whose oratory Cioran, at the outset of *Précis*, sees as definitive (Cioran, 2011, 4). Beckett was aware that pessimism arose as an 'imminent' consequence of hedonism and eudaemonism – the belief that everything in morals and ethics tends towards pleasure and happiness. As Hegesias maintained, in the 'chasm' between aim and achievement lay 'the annihilating consequence' of this belief, pessimism. Beckett also here provides himself with a detailed history around the major figures relating to ancient scepticism, under a general definition of the term as meaning 'All objective knowledge and absolute truth denied. Withdrawal of wise man into himself' (Beckett, 2020, 109–10).

In delineating the three phases of the early history of scepticism, Beckett seems most taken with, or at least to extrapolate upon, the fact that 'Our faculties cannot furnish us with information concerning essence of phenomena and our relations to them, but only concerning the relations of phenomena to one another.'[48] This not-knowing, or the impossibility of knowing, as Beckett noted, led early sceptics such as Pyrrho to concede the impossibility of forming an opinion, or of taking any action whatsoever. In turn, such irresolvability induces a state of 'ataraxy', that absolute calmness which is the only possible happiness, which can occur only in this state of 'non-committal condition of suspense' (Beckett, 2020, 197–8). This is the state Beckett's characters, from early,

---

[48] A similar recognition strikes in Cioran's *La chute dans le temps*, where the more intense the desire for knowledge becomes, the more humanity is rendered 'à côté' 'to one side of or outside' things (Cioran, 2011, 525).

through *Texts for Nothing*, till late, desire but never achieve (and that ataraxy for which Cioran says in *L'inconvenient d'être né* that he would give the whole universe and all of Shakespeare for one grain of; Cioran, 2011, 748).

More telling within the Beckettian mode of thinking, perhaps, are the uncertainties which the destabilisation between subject and object within scepticism, or perception and judgment, establishes. As the *'Philosophy Notes'* further extrapolate debates in this area, Beckett writes that the Sceptics' perception in every instance of an 'equilibrium of reasons' for holding any one opinion or response as against another 'excludes a distinction between true and false. (Eleatic element in Pyrrhonism)', and potentially sets in train a 'regressus ad infinitum' (Beckett, 2020, 201–2). This is the notorious 'breakdown of the object' for the perceiver, as signalled by Beckett from his reading in 'Recent Irish Poetry' of 1934 (Beckett, 1983, 70). This 'breakdown' variously developed through all of his fictions including, as we have seen, the unresolvable scepticism amidst which the narrator or narrators of *Textes pour rien* discover themselves. As Beckett's self-created history of philosophy avers, though, this time via Carneades, *both* the 'regressus' and the 'suspense' of ataraxy are equally impractical for 'the conduct of life'. Therefore, later sceptics adopted 'PROBABILISM', a kind of path of least contradiction or resistance as a 'modus vivendi' (Beckett, 2020, 204). Whence the habits of the Belacqua of 'Dante and the Lobster', through to the rituals and perambulations of such as 'M.', the male figure in *Ghost Trio*.

The *'Philosophy Notes'* also show a Beckett aware that, at least by the time of the Kantian tradition, scepticism had tended to become equated with nihilism – an element from the Presocratics and Democritus towards which, as Shane Weller has suggested, Beckett was particularly sympathetic (Weller, 2008, 323–4). The absolute equation of scepticism and nihilism for the Kantians, however, rendered it redundant, as they sought a priori conceptions towards the world – scepticism seemed to them, in fact, too grounded within the world. Beckett's *'Philosophy Notes'* are massively and exhaustingly elaborate in delineating all aspects of Kantianism whilst also frequently dismissive and exasperated by its transcendentalisms and idealisms. Against this tone of anti-relativism and anti-scepticism during the Kantian phase of philosophy, it is only perhaps when Beckett begins following the thinking of 'dear Arthur' Schopenhauer that the mood momentarily changes, especially around the latter's version of 'metaphysical pessimism':

This metaphysical pessimism Schopenhauer reinforces with hedonistic principle. Human life the perpetual flow between willing and attaining. But to will is pain. Hence pain is the positive affect, and pleasure only its removal. Hence pain must predominate in the world that is will (447).

In the drift of the history briefly traced here out of Beckett's own version, this 'positive affect' seems the most 'human' possibility – it induces 'sympathy' as a palliative, but also counteracts the idealism his *'Philosophy Notes'* so baulk at as the keynote of philosophy after Kant.[49]

It is only with Schopenhauer that something of that ancient 'ataraxy' is restored, in other words. This is, for Beckett, 'irrationalism' without 'the religious element': Schopenhauer 'found happiness of aesthetic condition in suspension of the will to live, in the activity of pure will-less subject of knowledge' (437).[50] But here again is limitation, since 'Philosophy of Schopenhauer has no use for history, which only presents facts' (447). Schopenhauer's sense of the pain of all willing, and of its inevitability *in* the world, discovers an aesthetics which in turn has 'no use' *for* the world, establishing that kind of endless oscillation found in Beckettian turns such as 'Imagination Dead Imagine'. Beckett's pre-War *'Philosophy Notes'* break off as he is launching into an account of Nietzsche's thinking, with what he describes as Nietzsche's continuous 'thirsts for boundless unfolding in action'. It is almost as though Beckett is exhausted and disgusted by further attempts, in the nineteenth century, to resuscitate philosophical history through such concepts as the 'Superman'. The nineteenth century itself, Beckett writes in his few sentences on the last of the philosophers in his *Notes*, was an age 'satisfied no longer by superpersonal values of the intellectual, aesthetic and moral' (475). By that point, all systems and concepts had collapsed into themselves and were vulnerable only to the extreme personality of such as Nietzsche.

The trajectory of Beckett's *'Philosophy Notes'* shares something similar to the priorities of Cioran's version of philosophical history, therefore, and Cioran clearly understood something of Beckett's attitudes intuitively.[51] On hearing of

---

[49] A reflection on scepticism early in *Cahiers* would suggest that Cioran might have demurred; *his* scepticism resists assault from his beliefs, he says – and also from his 'velléités metaphisiques', his weak inclinations towards the metaphysical (Cioran, 1997, 24). Perhaps as a consequence, Schopenhauer only flitters through Cioran's writings, despite his recollection that he studied him intensely as a student, and that Schopenhauer's aphorisms might have primed his own later taste for them (Cioran, 2011, 1253). Schopenhauer features as a kind of pre-Freudian for his interest in sexuality, or, alongside Nietzsche, as a leading philosopher on love and music – but little else (238, 1072).

[50] Schopenhauer is cast, alongside Nietzsche, in the role of inducing irrationalism to become the 'zone' of thinking and philosophy, from the outset of Cioran's writings in French (Cioran, 2011, 1254).

[51] Conversely, the *'Philosophy Notes'* and other of Beckett's pre-War note-snatchings show his comparative immunity to some figures key to Cioran's version of the history of philosophy. In numerous places in Cioran's writings and interviews, for example, he attests to the significance to him of Pascal, second only to the Presocratics in importance for him, and a crucial precursor in terms of the form Cioran's philosophy later takes (Cioran, 1995, 41). In *La tentation*, Pascal is identified as 'la nôtre', one of our own, because of his predictive sense of terror at the abyss (Cioran, 2011, 391). Beckett's *'Philosophy Notes'*, however, are mute on Pascal beyond giving

the award of the Nobel Prize to Beckett in 1969, for example, Cioran's *Cahiers* immediately feels sympathy for what such exposure will mean for Beckett, so proud a man. But the news also conjures the ghost of the tradition and a sense of shared attitude towards it, as Cioran nominates him 'Beckett ou l'anti-Zarathoustra, [...] l'apothéose du sous-homme' [the anti-Zarathoustra, [...] apotheosis of the under-man]. On the next page of his notebooks, Cioran then mulls further about the ideas of the 'insupportable' Nietzsche, clearly taking up again his thoughts about Beckett's award. There is no such thing as a 'surhomme', 'over-man', Cioran asserts; when we are born, we tear up our origins or roots – but only the harder to fall back into them, lower than ever before (Cioran, 1997, 753–4). Cioran's opposition to Nietzsche is consistent, even as Nietzsche's influence is evident in many ways; right back in 1957, at the outset of *Cahiers*, he dismisses such thinking and makes his own inclination obvious: 'je leur préfère les sages et les sceptiques, les "*non-inspirés*"' [I prefer to Nietzsche's writings the sages and sceptics, those "uninspired"] (107).

Cioran's entire self-characterisation as 'anti-philosophe' from *Précis de décomposition* onward, in fact, depends upon a kind of Schopenhauerian response to German idealism: 'Je me suis détourné' [I turned away] from philosophy when he found it impossible to find any 'aucun faiblesse humaine' [any human weakness] in Kant or any tone of human misery (46). These excluded accents of pain and sorrow, as a means to determine choices within the history of philosophy, must have struck Beckett on his first reading of *Précis*, and perhaps fuelled his determination to reread it. His own careful and scrupulous tracing of the history of philosophy down to Nietzsche had confirmed him in a similar scepticism towards human possibility and an awareness of the fallacy within writing which established man as in some way the measure.

But the '*Philosophy Notes*' do not signal this history as the only strand of potential concurrence between Beckett and Cioran. Cioran notably casts Beckett in his 'Quelques Rencontres' at some such limit as that one at which he places Nietzsche – *the limit*, or the 'extreme, the impasse'; that, for Cioran, is the basis of Beckett's endurance and heroism (Cioran, 2011, 1193). In interviews, Cioran extrapolated upon this concept for him of 'limit', associating it with 'une crise religieuse' he had undergone when aged twenty-five, a 'crise' although Cioran was and remained a non-believer. As a result, Cioran read all of

---

cursory dates and blandly listing him amongst those who used mathematics to underpin their sceptical ideas (Beckett 2020, 303, 311). There are a few quotations from the *Pensées* in the '*Whoroscope*' Notebook, so Beckett had read it in the 1930s (Beckett, UoR MS 3000, 70). Beckett in 1973 added a translation from one of the *Pensées* to his poetic sequence 'Long after Chamfort', after buying a second-hand copy during a stay in Tangier – but beyond that, little else (Beckett, 2012, 200, 440).

the Saints, but his concurrent and lifelong propensity to insomnia also reiterated his sense that 'on vit totalement seul'. 'Quand l'univers est évacué', he continues, 'vous touchez à une sorte de limite' [One lives totally alone [. . .] when the universe is emptied, you reach a kind of limit]. For a 'non-croyant' 'c'est ce qu'on appelle Dieu' [it is called God for non-believers]. In this state, Cioran claims, he came to understand 'vraiment la mystique', mysticism truly, and to understand particularly Master Eckhart, who spoke also 'de Dieu comme une sorte de limite' [of God as a kind of limit] (Cioran, 1995, 89).

'Limit', the word associated with Beckett, therefore, for Cioran, carries a specific charge, ranging from the personal experience of insomnia (underlying perhaps the late-night rambles and encounters with Beckett), through to his interest in the history of mysticism within philosophy, which gives his work its uniqueness from those amongst his first writings in Romanian, translated as *Tears and Saints*.[52] Beckett too, of course, was deeply imbued in that tradition including Eckhart, as was confirmed as late as a 1977 conversation reported by Charles Juliet (Juliet, 2009, 41). And, in turn, in the concluding paragraph of his appreciation of Beckett, 'Quelques Rencontres', when seeking an encapsulating praise for him, Cioran notably links Beckett to the definition of 'un homme noble' provided by both Eckhardt and Nietzsche (Cioran, 2011, 1195).

Beckett's '*Philosophy Notes*' are particularly eloquent about that mystical tradition, in ways that establish its potential within his later practice. To sketch only the thread around Eckhart, for example, we can see the kind of issues emerging with which Beckett and his characters centrally battle. Beckett wrote in the *Notes* that it is the intellect which 'determines the will' in the mystic tradition – the will which so focuses Schopenhauer's thinking and, subsequently, Beckett's interest in him. 'Intellect is the supremus motor, the source (Eckhart) even of Minne. This is intellectualistic determinism.' But this in turn creates a 'Problem of Individuality', as a subsection of this self-created history then has it: 'The Neo-Platonic intellectualism, in whatever form it appeared from Augustine to Meister Eckhart, was necessarily inclined to contest metaphysical self-subsistence of individual'. This challenge and 'problem' has the effect, as the '*Philosophy Notes*' taken following Beckett's sources have it, of a recursion: 'Eckhart and Transcendentalists have much in common – transposition of outer to inner, location of world in Gemüth'

---

[52] Cioran reconciled his sense of the link between scepticism and mysticism in interviews, pointing to the way that all saints confront an 'abyss' of doubt, and jump *across*; mystics remain passive before the abyss (Cioran, 1995, 155). David Wheatley has claimed that Cioran's understanding of the history around the saints is deeply indebted to 'Nietzsche's flushing out of the will to power behind Christian renunciation' (Wheatley, 2013, 48).

(Beckett, 2020, 278, 281, 423).[53] Beckett shared with Cioran, then, a thorough grounding in awareness that the mystics established 'the limit' for unbelievers and others as that place where, in Cioran's portrait of Beckett, all must and might begin. For both writers, the mystic tradition is embedded within the philosophical tradition from ancient Greece; its origins resonate through much of their thought and writing.

2.2 Philosophy in the Moment

Correlative to his sense of the value of those who step outside of daily 'business', Cioran's philosophy is fraught with a sense of the way the contemporary moment casts us all adrift: 'Le conscience occupe le vide qui suit l'érosion de l'existence par l'esprit; [...] la "réalité" [...] s'évanouit à l'approche du moindre doute' [Consciousness occupies that void which follows mind's breaking down of existence, [...] "reality" [...] vanishes when the least doubt hoves into view] (Cioran, 2011, 90–1). Mind, and thinking itself under this condition, has become corrosive or superficial, constantly caught between opposing knowledges towards 'reality'. As Cioran's writing develops through the 1950s and beyond, this alertness to the contemporary corrodes Cioran's texts and sees him seeking new forms in ways that are illuminating when thinking about Beckett's work as it took new shape across a similar period. This section will therefore pursue the nuance in Cioran's progression towards a new sense of form, in order to focus on consideration of Beckett's texts across the later 1950s and into the 1960s. For Beckett too, as he told Tom Driver, was impelled at around this point to seek a 'new form', one that now 'admits the chaos' of experience (Graver and Federman, 1979, 220).

As with his entering of the voice of the métèque cited earlier in this Element, Cioran is consistent throughout *Précis* in a practice of positioning in quotation marks the views of 'those' who carry through or expand upon the positions stated in uncited sentences and statements within each subsection. So, in 'La Corde', the rope, the opening short section of the last part of the book, we are given the 'speech' of someone whose 'confidence' the 'authorial narrator' of all of the book no longer recalls hearing. Nonetheless, the confidence is quoted in full, and ends '"tu es né pour te pendre comme tous ceux qui dédaignent un réponse à leurs doutes"' ["you are born to hang yourself like everyone who does not grant any answer for their doubts"] (Cioran, 2011, 138). Vladimir and Estragon might agree. In a text which has early established that 'nous n'existons

---

[53] Gemüth: 'the mind as the seat of the feeling and sentiments.' This latter reversion to thinking about Eckhart occurs interestingly quite late in the '*Philosophy Notes*', as Beckett's history mulls the break between 'thought and being' in the Kantian tradition.

qu'en tant que nous souffrons' [we exist only to the extent that we suffer], suicide, as 'La corde' posits, is perhaps what we are really born for (and not just by hanging, but also by throwing oneself from a window, according to Cioran's speaker, as Beckett's eponymous Malone thinks he might too) (27).

Précis, like all of Cioran's subsequent writing, is written in the shadow of the allure of suicide – but it is vital that such topics are given their expression via the 'quoted voices' of anonymous fellow-feelers to that persuasion in the main text.[54] Cioran's sense of modern consciousness as floating in a void, distinct from 'reality', is, in other words, enacted by the procedures of *Précis*. At key points, the text either 'quotes' or dramatises the perceptions of unnamed 'others' – the métèque, the despairingly suicidal – or puts other parts of the argument in paragraphs contained by brackets. These many instances create, as it were, texts within, or alongside, or against, the main text, philosophy in different modes, a congregation of possible attitudes, some in agreement, some in disagreement, but none of which predominates. The texts disturbingly, and without comment or explanation, enact the scepticism they advocate, as Beckett's syntax in *Texts* involves the reader in those losses of direction it otherwise describes. Both writers' works from this point are not simply *about* scepticism, but *are* sceptical whilst confronting the reality of it being impossible to prove or say that this is the case. To this extent, they establish a stance that both reflects the breakdown of coherent understandings and critiques them by exaggerating and demonstrating them – for philosophical and, in Adorno's sense, for political effect.

This all amounts, for Cioran in *Précis* and later, to a modern 'acedia' or (the term he applies more frequently in this regard) 'aboulia', 'stagnation de organs, cette hébétude des facultes', acedia such as that found in the hearts of those deserted by God (Cioran, 2011, 70). These 'stilled organs, stupefied senses', are something with which Cioran's despair as registered in *Cahiers* is also fraught, as in spring 1966's 'mon désespoir vient presque uniquement de mon aboulie' [my despair derives almost solely from my aboulia]. However much Cioran also registers in the same day's note an ambition to 'do' or 'make' something despite himself, through a conflict of theory with actuality the melancholy tone persists (Cioran, 1997, 352). Aboulia was, however, to become a key diagnosis in Cioran's published writings, a more broadly applicable diagnosis than the 'acedia' registered in *Précis*. Such ideas coalesce later in *La tentation*, when Cioran characteristically turns to thinking about the mystical tradition in both

---

[54] An interview of 1978 found Cioran at his most eloquent on the idea of suicide and its importance for his work; it allows him to 'sustain his life and enables him to break from feelings of slavery' (Cioran, 1995, 32).

Western and Eastern consciousness. He claims that we are only capable of fully living insofar as we struggle 'pour en briser les formes apparantes' [to break the forms of things before us]. 'L'ennui, le désespoir, l'aboulie' [boredom, despair, aboulia] all provide prompts to make this break with what constrains us, but only if each of them is also experienced as fully as possible (376–7). If we fully immerse in modern boredom, despair, aboulia, lack of will, in other words, some reaction might occur within us that forces us 'to break' with those models and patterns to which we are born.[55] Again, reason must be silenced. The tradition of saints and mystics, subject of Cioran's earlier *Tears and Saints*, provides ample examples of such 'breaking'. But, in *La tentation*, Cioran is not seeking to recover that lost Christian possibility.[56] What matters now are 'nos sensations, leur intensité et leurs vertus' [our sensations, their intensity and virtues], which throw us into ecstasy or dementia, 'une folie non sacrée' [unholy madness] (377).[57]

That linking of ennui to aboulia also throws us back from late in *La tentation* to early in *Précis*, where, in writing of the dislocations of time in the modern world, time without even the appearance of content or significance, it is 'Celui qui ne connait point l'ennui' [those who know nothing of boredom] who are the true children of the world, the remaining innocents (Cioran, 2011, 13). Cioran's first two books in French, in other words, posit a continuing Baudelairean sickness as all that enables us to know where we are, and all that might prompt us to resist and break the old forms, create the new. However, for *La tentation*, it is clear that every lapse into modernity is essentially a matter of adopting a particular style which is in turn endlessly proliferating. If 'pulvériser l'acquis' [to pulverise all the past (all the precursors)], reduce it to dust, is the vogue of 'l'esprit moderne', 'the modern spirit', and reason is dying in philosophy and the arts, that only leads to 'imprecision' in all things, including scepticism itself. We no longer measure doubt against certainties, but against 'd'autres doutes plus *consistants*' [more established doubts], in some endless spiral. As we have already established, French is perhaps, according to Cioran, particularly geared to this happening. As such, all writing becomes both a style, a mask, over this abyss, and 'un aveu', a testament or unknowing witness to the disconcertment of

---

[55] James Farrugia maintains that for Cioran it is the 'fear of boredom' and the 'horror' revealed by it that drive humans towards history (Farrugia, 2015, 221–2).

[56] *Le mauvais démiurge*, in fact, attributes 'aboulia' as an attitude specific to Christianity in resisting the kinds of awakening pursued by Eastern religions (Cioran, 2011, 682). David Wheatley has some good words to say about the 'metaphors' offered to Cioran by the mystical tradition and their correlatives in Beckett's work (Wheatley, 2013, 54).

[57] Cioran's discourse around this aspect conjures memories of Beckett's response when prompted about the mystics by Charles Juliet, confirming that he 'likes' their 'burning illogicality . . . the flame . . . the flame' (Juliet, 2009, 41).

the writer (352–3).[58] The relentlessness of the writing itself, its refusal of compromise with its audience, a refusal often aggressively rendered, is aimed to performative effect, to cause the audience to seek what Cioran would see as not just change, but active liberty from modern subservience.

Strikingly, when read with Beckett in mind, it is the unemployed, or beggars, as we have seen, who are idealised as witnesses within Cioran's first two books. Beggars and the homeless or cast out are those who resist travails around language in late history, or who resist in exemplary ways simply by not conforming. Towards the end of *Précis*, a beggar asking for small change in a city is compellingly compared to someone paused, 'attendre une réponse du silence de l'univers' [waiting for an answer from out of the universal silence] (53). The opening essay in *La tentation* then expands upon the comparison in a different tenor, enjoining the reader to 'contemplate' 'un mendiant' a beggar, since beggars 'ne ment ni ne se ment', neither 'lie nor lie to themselves'; what they believe, if they have any beliefs, they embody them, rather than speaking about them (and so lying) (268). Once again, Cioran's fixing upon those who seem deliberately to have stepped outside the otherwise valueless and contentless contemporary moment, simply to wait, links poverty, the ascetic (whether chosen or enforced), with honesty, but also with the mystics' attitude to being.

Whatever the shared conceptions between the Beckett of *Molloy* or the novellas *The Expelled, The Calmative*, and *The End* (with its own suicide), or of the early plays, and the Cioran who valorises the beggar as a kind of 'bare man' at this moment, there are sentences too in *Texts/Textes* when the speaker seems to be mounting the kinds of resistance against modern aboulias similarly figured by Cioran.[59] We find the speaker at the start of Text III, for example, accumulating limbs and a body, to 'say it's me', 'It's enough to will it, I'll will it' (Beckett, 2010a, 11). This after acknowledging that 'all is false', 'there is no one', so we can all rest as 'dupes'. The Text's coming-into-body as itself, in other words, is achieved through confronting the reality of the impossibility of saying true. The same un-illusion recurs to the court clerk or scribe posited as the narrator at the opening of Text V, who is embroiled in taking dictation in

---

[58] Cioran's *Cahiers* contains an inadvertently humorous account of yet another late night-encounter and drink with Beckett on 3 October 1966, during which Cioran admitted to writer's block attributable, he felt, to the way his interest in Eastern religions made him 'anathesthetized' even to his own deepest concerns. Beckett is reported to have patted him on the shoulder, as you would to someone lost, Cioran thinks, and as both an expression of sympathy and reassurance that it will be all right! (Cioran, 1997, 413).

[59] For Alain Badiou, this is the pivot which sets Beckett against that humanism which envisages a 'tragic devastation' to have occurred in history, for which he is so often (and wrongly, in Badiou's view) praised. Rather, for Badiou, it is when his characters reach that 'extreme point of devastation' that they '*succeed*' since they escape 'all the disastrous ornamentations of circum-stance' (Badiou, 2003, 3).

a case against themselves and who describes willing 'in vain to see there can't be any willing' (21). The French original is more self-cancelling, even suicidal, around this resistance, 'je me tue vouloir voir' [I kill myself to will to see] (Beckett, 1958, 146).

What is finally notable in this spectrum of conjunctions and concurrencies between Beckett and Cioran is how such shared senses of inertia in this modern moment determine that word which seems to have been most shared between them once the two writers become personally well acquainted in the early 1960s. *Précis* punctures all ideas of 'a new life' by noting that all inspiration and passions are now degraded; as a consequence, 'L'authenticité d'une exist-ence consiste dans sa propre ruine' [The truthfulness of any existence is made up of its own ruin] (Cioran, 2011, 67–8). The concept clearly sustained some currency for them both: Beckett responded to *Le mauvais démiurge* (1969), which he had begun reading on its publication, by writing in a letter to Cioran, 'Dans vos ruines je me sens à l'aise' [in your ruins I feel at ease] (Beckett, 2016b, 157). Tellingly, when Cioran noted Beckett's response to *Démiurge* in his *Cahiers*, he substituted Beckett's 'à l'aise' with 'à l'abri', as though Beckett was finding shelter against the storm amidst Cioran's ruins, rather than simply feeling comfortable there (Cioran, 1997, 715).

And, in turn, such uncertainties seem to play around the dialogue the two writers had in January 1974 about how best to translate the title of Beckett's already published *Sans/Lessness* of 1969–70, the text which begins in English, 'Ruins true refuge long last' (Beckett, 2010a, 129; 2016b, 355–6).[60] Beckett's headnote to the Calder edition of *Lessness* of 1970 notably makes play between 'refuge' and 'refugee' – the collapse of the former impelling the 'ensuing situation' of the latter (Nixon, 2010, xvii). The intricate combinations and recombinations of Beckett's text dramatise, as it were, the process towards that 'situation', particularly as it effects itself on the body and the mind. In the closing movement of the piece, we find a fading towards blankness, as 'No sound not a breath same grey all sides earth sky body ruins' integrates flesh and circumstance. Slightly later, 'light of reason all gone from mind' – the anti-Enlightenment measure of all this is confirmed (131, 132).[61] When read

---

[60] This dialogue, significantly about the most correct word or title for Beckett's piece, and one moving from Latin to French to English, clearly had importance for Cioran at least within the two writers' connection (Cioran, 2011, 1191). According to the BDMP pages on Beckett's library, Cioran wrote something about it when dedicating *L'inconvenient d'être né* in 1973 (Beckett, 2016b). Cioran also repeats his account of this dialogue in the memoir of Beckett collected in *Aveux et anathèmes*. The image of ruins and refuge recurs in *How It Is*, in many ways a precursor text for the extrapolations and variations of *Lessness*, as we will see.

[61] The late text 'neither' expands the purgatorial aspect of this, situating itself between two 'lit refuges' and rendering the concept of home 'unspeakable' (Beckett, 2010a, 167).

alongside Cioran's *Le mauvais démiurge* (1969), with its own 'ruins', according to Beckett, aspects of *Lessness*, and the conversation Beckett had with Cioran over its French titling, coalesce. Essentially reprising many themes from earlier in his writings, Cioran in *Le mauvais démiurge* nevertheless expands, through his enquiry into the nature of the relation of humans to gods at this point in time, upon that 'personal' identification and 'confessional' element in his philosophy, in ways that might galvanise the 'je me sens' aspect of Beckett's reading.[62]

Cioran's 1969 text indeed bears some mark of the conversations he otherwise reported himself as having had with Beckett, most notably in its several references to the fourth Book of Jonathan Swift's *Gulliver's Travels*.[63] This Book, and the reportedly somewhat misogynist response to it by Beckett, forms one facet of the conversation between Cioran and Beckett reported in *Aveux*, since Beckett is rereading that fourth Book of *Gulliver* at the recounted moment (Cioran, 2011, 1194). Beckett displays, according to Cioran, a relish for the part of Swift's novel where Gulliver recoils from his wife on his return from the land of the horses – or, as Gulliver himself reports, 'when I began to consider, that by copulating with one of the yahoo species I became a parent of more, it struck me with the utmost shame, confusion, and horror' (Swift, 1976, 234). There are clear links between this and the general atmosphere of *Le mauvais démiurge*, with its sexual despair and anti-procreative energies.[64] This is most notably so when, in the essay 'Paléontologie', Cioran includes Swift alongside Baudelaire

---

[62] Beckett's interest in the biographical and confessional nature of writing configures aspects of his 1930s note-snatching, with the regular inclusion of brief biographies and extensive bibliographies – but it also informs the focus of those notes, as, for example, in the dwelling upon Goethe's *Dichtung und Wahrheit* (Nixon, 2006, 262, 269).

[63] Cioran's *Histoire et utopie* had earlier cited Swift's novel as proof that the only readable versions of literary utopia were those that were either written in jest, for fun, or out of misanthropy (Cioran, 2011, 493). In terms of Beckett's 'light of reason all gone from mind', of course, this fourth Book of *Gulliver's Travels* is particularly pertinent and links to both Cioran's and Beckett's concerns around language. The 'master' horse or Houyhnhnm frequently mocks the diminished display of reason amongst humans demonstrated through Gulliver's account of England to him. We are told that amid the dream of reason represented by the horses '*doubting* or *not believing*' do not exist, and it is impossible, because irrational '*to say the thing which was not*' – to use words which do not absolutely represent the things spoken of. Gulliver struggles to help the 'master' understand that in human speech, words are often used for '*false representation*' (Swift, 1976, 193).

[64] Cioran's *Cahiers* comments on his reading of Swift from about June 1964; in February 1969, he mentions having heard this passage about Gulliver's return from the Houyhnhnms in an English recording, finding it even more forceful than when he read it in French and noting Swift's 'horror' at sex and his unique sense of shame (Cioran, 1997, 234, 236, 686). Cioran's other admired reading in literature in English notably speaks to his yearning for a settled, even romanticised first place. He clearly loved the work of Emily Bronte, relished visiting Haworth, and notes Bronte's anguish at having to leave it for Brussels (199, 673). In poetry, his true favourite was Emily Dickinson (Cioran, 1995, 152).

and the Buddha when sketching a history of disgust at the perishability and disease-ridden actuality of the 'flesh' as an obsession which links ancient religions East and West through Christianity. Flesh is 'incurable nothingness, a fiction which has degenerated into a calamity' (Cioran, 2011, 646–7). Alternatively, Beckett's 'little body' in *Lessness* does not so much decompose, but rather becomes integrated within the decomposition all around it, or is notably (from the perspective of the Cioran) subsumed, including in finding sex quelled: 'Little body little block genitals overrun' is the last we see of it (Beckett, 2010a, 132).

2.3 The Fragment, the Aphorism, and the Philosophical[65]

Once again, as stated, for Cioran, such disgusts are inextricable from the approach to philosophy which has resounded within his work from the start – yet now the mask, as it were, has melded onto the face. In the telling gambit of his 'Rencontres avec le suicide' essay from *Le mauvais démiurge*, Cioran rounds off with the flourish that he had, 'pendant longtemps' for a long time now worked through the theory of the man-outside-everything, separate man, or man apart. But now 'je le suis devenu, je l'incarne maintenant' [I have become him, incarnate him] (Cioran, 2011, 675). The net outcome, as the more aphoristic final section of the book makes clear, is direct identification. 'What remains' of a philosopher is his 'temperament', which makes him forget '*himself*', yield to contradiction (scepticism in other words), and free himself from all attention to or concern for coherence (722). It is as though, as Cioran's writing developed across the 1960s, he was increasingly reconfirmed in the role he had cast for himself within the drift of the time. Beckett's increasingly abandoned 'refugee' output from this era suggests a similar course if seen from that perspective.

Significant, also, within the sense of 'ruins' as some kind of version of a late modernist consciousness, and as a way of establishing further conjunctions between the prose writings of Beckett and Cioran through to the 1970s, is the way that, for *both*, the inextricable and performative link between consciousness and style increasingly took on a formal implication. Beckett's 'Pour finir encore'/'For to end yet again', after all, spanned the time of the late 1960s and *Lessness*, with an afterlife into the mid-1970s. That text makes us watch a 'first change of all', as a 'fragment comes away from mother ruin and with slow fall scarce stirs the dust'. As the disintegration progresses, we watch the bizarrely

---

[65] Andrew Hui has pointed to the interchangeability of the aphorism and the fragment within the history of Western philosophy – for him, the aphorism 'oscillates between the fragment' and the system which philosophy looks for or looks to build (Hui, 2019, 7).

coined 'bump of habitativity', or love of home, 'yearn' skywards, before, like Milton's Satan, this 'expelled' plummets amidst 'his' ruins (Beckett, 2010a, 152). The mothering of the ruin here determines a sterile and damned birthing of her son. As we have seen that urge to break up form, 'briser les formes' as both content and formal characteristic of the text is mapped by Cioran onto a modern tendency to turn everything of the past into dust. But that sense of formal possibility as a particular degradation in post-War history seems also to have become embedded as a formal necessity and opportunity as Cioran's thinking developed.

In late 1963, after an entry in *Cahiers* when he again meditated on the history of philosophy as a series of phases which then recede from Hegel through Schopenhauer, Cioran seems to draw implication for his own work in the next entry: 'Je dois revenir au fragment proprement dit. [. . .] Mon esprit [. . .] ne peut pas "construire"' [I have to come back to the fragment, to speak true. My spirit [. . .] cannot "build" things, make them] (Cioran, 1997, 196). Once again, this sense of lassitude, not being able to get beyond, as it were, what Cioran calls here 'd'ébauches', sketches or drafts, the first form in which his thoughts come to him or to build them into more sustained structures. And *Cahiers* keeps coming back to this, perhaps because of its own almost diurnal notational mode; in January 1969, for instance, we hear that 'le fragment' is his 'natural mode of expression', 'je suis né pour le fragment' [I was born for it] (686).[66]

This process of writerly degradation or discontinuity then becomes a structural facet of Cioran's later writings. *Le mauvais démiurge* (1969) and *Écartèlement* (1971) both set out with a series of essayistic pieces before increasingly in their final portions becoming paragraph- or sentence-length sections often divided by visual section markers. They present in this way more aphoristic, relatively random sets of thoughts. It is as though, in other words, we witness these texts decomposing as we read – or at least becoming only increasingly able to operate through shorter breaths. The aphoristic section of *Le mauvais démiurge* advertises this, coming as it does under the heading 'PENSÉES ÉTRANGLÉES', 'strangled thoughts'; 'ÉBAUCHES DE VERTIGE', something like 'vertiginous first drafts' heads the aphoristic later phase of *Écartèlement*. Cioran's last purely philosophical text, *L'inconvenient d'être né*, which Beckett acknowledged as 'fraternal' in 1973, is solely made up of brief aphorisms.

---

[66] The editorial material for Cioran's *Oeuvres* points to the fact that *Précis* was initially constructed of more than 200 brief essays and 'fragments' of variable length – Cioran's practice in making his first book seems, then, to have become an approach to reading the contemporary world (Cioran, 2011, 1302).

Some of these later books are suggestive more broadly about the development of Cioran's ideas *as* response to their moment of writing and publication: it is striking that *Ecartèlement*, a 1979 edition of which is in Beckett's library, for instance, contains a chapter 'Urgence du pire', the urgency of the worst, a reading of history as a kind of hurtle towards a disaster that never arrives. In August 1981, Beckett begins drafting *Worstward Ho*. Yet Cioran's sense of an increasingly formal implication around his philosophical understanding also seems to resonate. As Mark Nixon has noted when reflecting on Beckett's practice and publication of his 1964 'Faux Départs', one aspect of the 'experimentation' of Beckett's shorter prose at this period is that he allowed 'fragments' to be published – a practice that was to continue into his later career[67] (Nixon, 2010, xiii). With the exception of *Comment c'est* (1961), whose formal nature will form a point of discussion later in this Element, Beckett's work from the early 1960s (but looking backwards to the work of the late 1940s too) will consist of these briefer, often more broken-off forms. And extracts already given suggest that, for Beckett, 'fragments' figure also as expressive content within the later prose, effecting a disintegration within the text which might itself be read as fragmentary, as Section 3.1 will explore further.

At this stage, it is important to note an unspoken formal elision which underpins much in Cioran and which derives from an interest in a specifically French tradition shared by Beckett. Cioran's increasing deployment of the prose fragment as response to modernity seems concurrent with the aphoristic drive which also characterised his work from early to late.[68] Philosophically, that emphasis and practice might be taken to derive from Pascal, Schopenhauer, and Nietzsche, but Cioran was also aware of the literary inheritance on which he drew. Cioran rounds off his appreciation of Beckett, indeed, by noting Beckett's own recent generic shift, in rendering some of Chamfort's aphorisms into English verse – something almost inconceivable, Cioran maintains, given the 'squelettique' [skeletal] nature of Chamfort's prose. But Cioran sees this latest manoeuvre almost as a declaration of faith on Beckett's part. It provides further evidence, according to him, of the mysterious workings of inspiration in those

---

[67] Of course, Beckett did not only come to thinking about the fragment in the early 1960s – the third zone of Murphy's mind, for instance, contains 'forms becoming and crumbling into the fragments of a new becoming' (Beckett, 2009b, 72). The point, though, as for Cioran, is that the fragment increasingly becomes both mode and content of both writers' later works as their sense of alienation hardens.

[68] Cioran makes precisely this elision in an interview, where, in answer to a question about the consistent use of fragments in his writing, he points to the influence of 'des moralistes' he had read from his youth onwards – and adds that now (1982) they had taken over his writing. This is because aphorisms are appropriate to a civilisation which 'se désagrège', is falling apart, but also because he likes the illogic of aphorisms, which 'se détruisent les uns les autres' [mutually destroy each other] (Cioran, 1995, 77–8).

writers who are truly great, as well as proclaiming the essentially poetic nature of all of Beckett's work, whatever its genre (Cioran, 2011, 1194).

Chamfort, often alone, often paired with La Rochefaucauld, features in Cioran's writings from the outset, to the extent that, by the time of *L'inconvenient d'être né*, Cioran records the bursts of gratitude he feels both to Chamfort and to Job – albeit that, as he acknowledges, he feels those 'bursts' at ever-widening intervals (717). Several times in interviews, Chamfort, paired or otherwise, figures for Cioran as a way of relegating the often 'correct' but 'solitary' vision of a Nietzsche as an influence; Chamfort is closer to 'l'expérience vrai de l'homme' [humanity's true experience], 'homme' as necessarily connected to society and the times (Cioran, 1995, 57, 77, 251). That experience is now marked, as Cioran is concurrently hyper-aware, by the wars of the twentieth century. In an odd moment at the end of the opening 'lettre' to *Histoire et utopie*, the speaker ironically regrets that Paris has not been destroyed in either conflict since its physical continuation means he literally cannot move on to other places. Undestroyed, he has to endure the happiness of living there and is in danger of becoming identified with the city. Consoling himself, he recalls that Chamfort has noted that four-fifths of Parisians 'meurent de chagrin' anyhow – they 'die of grief' (Cioran, 2011, 445). The speaker maintains that the remaining fifth, of which he is part, have the same feelings; they simply lack knowledge '*de quoi*' of what they should die.

A section towards the end of *Précis de décomposition* made the motivation behind this speaker's tongue-in-cheek acquiescence towards Chamfort's assertion clear. In 'Dans le secret des moralistes', Cioran felt that the necessarily 'melancholy' attitude we must take to the universe means that all we have left to us are rare lightning bursts of joy: 'lorsque nous n'espérons plus que nous subissons la fascinations de l'espoir' [Only when we have given up on hope (is it) that we submit to hope's fascinations]. Truly bitter words, therefore, can only come from those whose sensibility is truly ulcerated; the viciousness of a La Rochefoucauld or a Chamfort derives from 'la revanche qu'ils prirent contre un monde taillé pour les brutes' [revenge against a world cut out for brutes] (Swift's Yahoos, perhaps) (148). In an aphorism, that burst of revenge is gleeful, an attack on false delicacy, and the mixture of seriousness and joyous spite in aphorisms, for Cioran, is therefore to be relished. Yet, when revenge against the nature of the world 'se traduit' 'translates itself' into a 'system', as it will, Cioran claims, then the name of that system is 'pessimism', 'cette *cruauté de vaincus*', 'cruelty of the defeated'. This is the revenge of those who have lost their place in history, the resentment of those whose thoughtfulness, perhaps their civilisation (in contrast to the 'brutes'), has been 'murdered'. Not far away from 'le venin' of this is the violence already registered in and through Cioran's writing, or that experienced by those in the constrained circumstance of Beckett's *The Lost Ones*.

Cioran's snatching of an aphoristic *mot* to set up his placing of La Rochefoucauld and Chamfort in *Précis* – 'lorsque nous n'espérons plus' [. . .] – is in the rhetorical field of the famous perception from the latter that Beckett marked on page 31 of his 1950 edition of Chamfort's *Maximes et Anecdotes*:

> L'espérance n'est pas qu'un charlatan qui nous trompe sans cesse, et, pour moi, le bonheur n'a commencé que lorsque je l'ai eus perdue. Je mettrais volontiers sur la porte du paradis le vers que le Dante a mis sur celle de l'enfer: 'Lasciata ogni speranza, voi ch'entrate.'[69]

Beckett's version of these words, 'Hope is a Knave', was then gathered with six other renditions of Chamfort maxims from those marked in Beckett's copy, together with one saying from Pascal, as part of the short sequence 'Long after Chamfort' in 1977 (they were complete by late 1973, and Beckett had already tried out draft versions in his correspondence to friends) (Beckett, 2012, 438). Although Cioran purports to wonder at the generic shift from Chamfort's prose to Beckett's English verse, in fact all Beckett has done is to adopt and adapt the rhyming couplet, staple of the literary period in English correlative to the time of Chamfort's writing, to contain his translated words.

In this regard, it is striking that, as Seán Lawlor and John Pilling mention in their notes to *The Collected Poems*, Beckett's 'sleep till death' – another of these versions from Chamfort – echoes in its fourth and last line lines 131–2 of Alexander Pope's *Epistle to Dr Arbuthnot*.[70] Beckett's denomination of our 'life disease' conflates Pope's comment on his own life course: 'The Muse but served to ease some friend, not wife, | To help me through this long disease, my life' (440). Pope's *Epistle* was itself assembled, as Pope acknowledged, or 'written by piece-meal many years' – constructed from previously completed fragments. The lines echoed by Beckett come in a passage which notoriously associates writing with Original Sin ('what sin to me unknown | Dipped me in ink') (Pope, 1993, 662). Behind Beckett's version of Chamfort's original

---

[69] This marking is pictured in the BDMP Library page for this edition (Beckett, 2016a). 'Hope is only a charlatan who lies to us endlessly, and, for me, happiness only begins once I've lost hope. I would willingly put on the gate of paradise what Dante put on Hell's gate, "Lose all hope you who enter here"' (my translation). Séan Lawlor and John Pilling, in their note to Beckett's English version of this maxim, recount that Beckett twice inscribed Chamfort's original French, nearly word perfectly, as dedication in two copies of *Fin de Partie/Endgame*, in 1967 and 1969 – as though the words encapsulated an atmosphere out of which the play was written, perhaps particularly with its outbursts of frustration (Beckett, 2012, 437–8).

[70] Frederik N. Smith points to the fact that this Pope work appeared on the curriculum at Trinity College during Beckett's time as a student (Smith, 2002, 12).

apothegm 'la mort est le rèmede', in other words, lies a whole complex of resonance which sounds through his technical and verbal choices in making this translation. That resonance, in its turn, speaks more widely to not just the life-view, but the kinds of writerly fascination and decision which determined Beckett's thinking from early to late in his career.

That formal decision to render Chamfort's prose as a variously imitated set of rhyming couplets in English renders a levity to the often over-earnest tones of the original, several times by stripping away the dogged circumstance out of which Chamfort derives his telling phrase. Chamfort's 'lead in' to his maxims, 'Quand on soutient . . . Quand on a été bien tourmenté', are both dropped as Beckett seizes on the chiming wit of the couplet (Beckett, 2012, 198). The alternately rhyming quatrain 'Hope is a Knave' (which exists in couplet versions in its drafts), the only 'longer' sally in the sequence, is also the most provocative in suggesting a sensibility caught in the parallel collapsed world of Cioran's version of Chamfort. Beckett's witty wordplay, suggesting that the speaker might 'grave' Dante's words on Heaven's (not Inferno's!) door, also conjures an inverted world close to that of Cioran's own *Le mauvais démiurge*, which Beckett had read three years before coming to his final version of 'Hope is a Knave'. The decadent world of excess civilisation, which Cioran felt to have driven on the revenge and venom of Chamfort and La Rochefaucauld, speaks now in Beckett's recasting as an angrier response to the moment (the speaker will 'strike' off Dante's slogan to 'grave' it).

Coming after the briefer and more fractured prose Beckett developed through the 1960s, 'Long after Chamfort' signals its weariness but also the bitterness behind its playful but pessimistic inversion of expectation, even its reversal of Dante. His contracted couplet versions extract the humorous possibility from the po-faced Chamfort originals, but do not disrupt the essential world view as they suggest its continued relevance. This practice of, as it were, carving a brief aphoristic phrase out of or amidst its larger context in the prose shows Beckett to have honed a technique that he had been evolving across the past decade and more, as his forms had become more contracted and inconsistent – that breaking which his mid-late prose shared, out of a similar tradition, with Cioran.

3 Form as Violence

3.1 *How It Is* and *Fizzles*, the Aphoristic and the Essayistic

The critical and theoretical consensus which focuses around *Comment C'est/ How It Is*, and the way it has been responded to by the few critics who have considered Cioran alongside Beckett hitherto, suggest it as *the* work which might present the most intent material for comparison between the two.

The editor of the critical-genetic edition of the novel, Édouard Magessa O'Reilly, makes a strong case that it is only here in Beckett's writing that fragmentation is truly his method – other late works often described as 'fragmentary' are in fact made up of an often pre-decided number of paragraphs (O'Reilly, 2001, x). In another vein around the formal nature of the work, Alain Badiou regards *How It Is* as creating the 'major transformation' in Beckett's career, one where he moves towards '*the figural poem of the subject's postures*'. In order to track 'the discontinuity' of those 'postures', the prose becomes 'segmented' into paragraphs constructed as 'musical units', which (rather loosely) Badiou seems to claim as 'poetic'.[71] Most notably, this segmentation of the text allows for the 'event' to enter the fictive surface, as, for Badiou, the narrator's encounter with Pim allows for the first time in Beckett's writing 'the instantaneous surprise of the Other'. The endless rehearsals of selfhood in the earlier texts are 'broken' in *How It Is*, and so, for the first time, an 'event' happens in and through the writing (Badiou, 2003, 15–16).

Badiou here might be taken to concur with the methodology of Pascale Casanova, which argues for a critical approach based on the fact that 'Beckett never stopped repeating how central formal preoccupations were for him' (Casanova, 2006, 86). *Comment C'est/How It Is* would seem to offer itself as the proof of this; the genetic account O'Reilly provided would confirm that it is with what he calls the 'ms/r' redrafting, the opening of space between blocks of French text, that Beckett makes one of his most radical gambits, when taken with the elisions in the phrases and dropping of punctuation within the blocks. (O'Reilly, 2001, xx).

Alternately, David Wheatley has argued that *How It Is* answers most fully to that interest of Beckett's shared with Cioran – mysticism, particularly as explored in Cioran's early text translated as *Tears and Saints*. Once again, this is not a matter of direct influence – *Tears and Saints* was not published until 1998 in English translation from the Romanian – but rather of parallel or comparative concerns and images. Wheatley sees in the 'gasping fragments' and expansive 'fragmenting' of *How It Is* 'pitiful screams of distress'. These are screams such as those emanating in Cioran's view from the saints, or here from the 'agony' of the main narrator, an agony shared with that of the 'desert fathers' (Wheatley, 2013, 51–2). The whole novel, from Wheatley's perspective,

---

[71] Claire Joubert has pointed to the problems of this view of Beckett in Badiou, in that 'his rethinking of ethics through the poetics of prose turns out to be the process where the ethical pathos of nihilism is simply reversed in an equally pathetic repositivisation of value'. Joubert does grant, however, that this simple reversal takes place through Badiou's fraught sense that it is at the end of history, as it were, the poets who have taken over what she calls 'the work of thought' from the philosophers – Mallarmé and Celan (with Hölderlin as 'visionary precursor'), in Badiou's view, along with Beckett (Joubert, 2012, 42, 44).

represents a solitary's attempt to commune with an absent God in a kind of tempered metaphysics which Cioran and Beckett are taken to share. The fragmentation in *How It Is*, in other words, serves for Wheatley a dramatic function; as with Cioran's bursts of insight or despair, the discontinuity of self and world functions to enter the pure cries of a lost consciousness *in extremis* (52).

From both strains of argument, the formal and the Cioran-like mystical or saintly, it is the metatextual aspects of *How It Is* that stand most prominently. It is at those moments that a 'metaphysical pessimism' seems to break the surface of the writing. In *Écartèlement*, Cioran points out that those states of mind or being in which the cause is identifiable are not fruitful; those which 'nous enrichissent' [add to us], are those which arrive 'sans que nous sachions pourquoi' [without our knowing the reason]. These Cioran identifies as 'états excessifs', states where joy or despondency 'menacent l'intégrité de notre esprit' [threaten the wholeness of our spirit] (Cioran, 2011, 984–5). *How It Is* seems to be such an 'état' in a double sense, excessive in its austere absoluteness as a place and space beyond, and, as such, one in which the threat to all integrity is most shadowed. So, in Part Three of *How It Is*,

> [...] I'm sorry again no one here knows himself it's the place
> without knowledge whence no doubt its peerlessness (Beckett, 2001, 159)

The non-knowing self in the not-knowing place. The apology glimmers with a possibility of address to an other (human or God) which shimmered more fully in an earlier French draft which inserted or had 'nous regrettons' before it emphatically became 'je regrette' (there was previously a lot of 'nous' and 'nos' around this section of Beckett's initial, French, drafts) (547).

'Peerlessness' is striking; Beckett's earlier goes at rendering the straight-faced 'son prix' in his final French version had been direct, 'worth', or 'great price' (722–3). 'Peerlessness' gives a greater literary decisiveness, perhaps, as it puts this moment of apology to the listener or reader within the orbit of Shakespeare phrases such as the Gentleman's comment in Act Five Scene I of *A Winter's Tale*, when speaking of Perdida: 'Ay, the most peerless piece of earth, I think,/That ere the sun shone on.'[72]

Where Shakespeare, as it were, celebrates the return to presence of some grace that had been thought forever lost, Beckett's sense of this earthly place is that it is peerless as a state of absolute exclusion, no one, without, no doubt. The reiterated apology in this fragment in a sense acknowledges the frustration of the thereby excluded reader or hearer, seeking precisely the kinds of return that

---

[72] Anthony Cordingley links 'peerlessness' to the other erasures which undermine 'the *ratio* of the "I"' as part of the inheritance from Stoicism in the novel (Cordingley, 2018, 94).

this text knows itself to be unable to give. As we have heard near the start of Part Three,

> [. . .] all that almost blank nothing to get out of it almost nothing nothing to
> put in that's the saddest that would be the saddest imagination
> on the decline [. . .] (131)

'Blanc' replaces an earlier 'vide' in a French draft in a literalisation which sees the text 'almost' recede into the whiteness of the page (507). The English 'blank' carries a kind of expressive thoughtlessness, where the French promotes the colour and nudges us towards the gap or gulf (another 'chasm' between aim and achievement, in 'pessimist' terms) in the page we have just crossed. The previous block of text has noted that time is breaking down, leaving only a few 'indelible' traces of lives lived, or 'lives crosses', as the English version has it, in a telling elision and concentration of the original French 'marquer une vie plusieurs des croix'. The repetition of 'saddest' in the quote is an addition to the French text and also to the first draft of Beckett's translation; for the imagination to decline is initially the 'saddest' thing, but in the final English text the imagination itself has become the actual saddest thing too.

As he works on the text and between drafts and languages, it is as though Beckett's awareness of a Cioran-like 'excessiveness', an over-larding of the implications of all of this, grows. The final English version only points us to the emotiveness relating to this 'place' or situation; it cannot redeem us from it. This is because the text itself declines and expands between the more sustained and the shorter, more aphoristic and proverbial possibilities: the next block of text here is the single line, 'or ascending heaven at last no place like it in the end'.[73] 'No place like it' is strikingly idiomatic; the French has a nice play after 'ciel', 'enfin que ça au fond', upwards and to the depths. An early English version had tried to mirror, in a displaced way, the verb in the French single-line phrase, 'monter' – no place 'to come up to it' (703).

The idiomatic 'no place like it', when struck upon, gives the phrase an aphoristic tinge in the English text. *How It Is*, in fact, is peppered with such Englishisms and also Irishisms, providing a rhythmic underpinning, often at key metatextual moments. In Part Two, for instance, we have a textual block to which Beckett has added the idiomatic 'je le dis comme je l'entends', which he renders blankly as 'I say it as I hear it' in English (122, 123, 495).[74] But then, in

---

[73] Hui, whose 'theory' of the aphorism frequently points out that the aphorism, the fragment, and the proverb overlap consistently, quotes a pertinent aphoristic phrase from Walter Benjamin: 'A proverb, one might say, is a ruin which stands on the site of an old story' (Hui, 2019, 74).

[74] As so often in the echo chamber of these middle and late Beckett texts, he is partly taking dictation from himself. In the final pages of *The Unnamable* we are told 'I say what I hear, I hear what I say, I don't know, one or the other' (Beckett, 2010b, 132).

the next block, we have as the opening phrase in French 'rien aussi bien sûr souvent rien malgré tout mort rose et tiéde', which the English renders proverbially as 'nothing too to be sure often nothing in spite of everything dead as mutton warm and rosy'. The punning on the Irishism 'to be sure' sets up the addition in the typescript translation 'as mutton', reinflecting the deadness of the French intonation towards the rosiness of the just killed and uncooked meat.

All of this is estranging, weirdly marooning the idiomatic, aphoristic amidst a seemingly airless and intractable situation. Much pivots in the novel around the first kind of not-knowing in this place contained in the first quotation just cited from the novel. Earlier in Part Two, for instance, recounting his times with his lover Pam Prim, the narrator seems literally to stumble when trying to find the words to tell her where he had looked in seeking out the holly with berries she so desired: 'one step forward two back', as he breaks off on another proverbial and idiomatic Irishism. But this only turns him back on himself, the irredeemable self, now adopting a seemingly posthumous account:

> my life above what I did in my life above a little of everything tried
> everything then gave up no worse always a hole a ruin always a crust [...] (101)

Hole, ruin. Additions in the French, trou, ruine, to replace the original singular 'toit de besoin', 'needful roof' (463). If the opening of Part Three accounts for Pim and his departure as his 'seeking out the true home', absolute, it is telling also that the Second Part of the novel frequently touches on that needed 'toit' with which émigré Cioran and Beckett were so ennervatedly familiar (131).

There is a rare moment, a brief paragraph in Cioran's *L'inconvenient d'être né*, where the speaker tells us in the present tense of his closing the curtains and waiting: 'En fait je n'attends rien, je me rends seulement *absent*' [I wait for nothing, I just make myself absent/an absence]. Freeing himself of the clogs of the mind, this speaker achieves a state of consciousness 'd'où le moi est évacué' [from where the I is voided], and, in peace, that consciousness which rests outside the universe (Cioran, 2011, 814). It is a meditative, meditational, moment, integral with Cioran's Buddhist interest.[75] But it is also striking that the moment can only occur in a room from which it is possible, however temporarily and flimsily, to block out the world. The next paragraph in the

---

[75] Cordingley identifies the 'Eastern sage' who oddly appears near the start of Part Two of *How It Is* with the Gautama Buddha (Cordingley, 2018, 64–5). Andy Wimbush notes Beckett's knowledge of Buddhism as one aspect of his quietism, and cross-refers this interest to Cioran (Wimbush, 2020, 179–81). A further way of thinking about this (in Cioran but also in Beckett) might be the American philosopher Stanley Cavell's pointing to those moments when 'the stillness of the text' amounts to 'the withholding of assertion', a self-containedness 'on which I have found the defeat of scepticism, and of whatever metaphysics is designed to overcome scepticism, to depend'. Cavell's suggestion is that such moments are 'interpretable politically' (Cavell, 1984, 51).

book sees Cioran's speaker implying that this is a rare possibility in history. He points to the 'poetry' by which the Middle Ages could take time to exorcise evil spirits from each named part of the body in turn, as though implying that this is no longer available as a ritual for the lodged modern speaker of the previous paragraph – and conjuring the speaker of Beckett's *Text* III, who contemplates decomposing one limb at a time. The narrator of Part Two of *How It Is*, however, is allowed no such time of lodging or shutting out, since there is 'always' 'a hole a ruin' amidst the frequent blanks and variously broken text.[76]

As we are told at one point, 'les blancs sont les trous', 'the gaps are the holes' through which we see a disillusioned speaker returned 'home to my native land to die in my twenties' (Beckett, 2001, 108, 109). But now, or in the seemingly posthumous now of the narrator, he goes out having hidden by day, 'a hole a ruin | land strewn with ruins all ages' (111). The apocalyptic vision seems to destroy the speaker, who in an addition to one typescript is made to plead 'que faire que faire', 'what to do?' (478). That apocalyptic vision had been pre-empted in Beckett's works by the opening image of 'Afar a Bird', 'Ruinstrewn land' (Beckett, 2010a, 143). Yet, in the ambiguous rhythm of *How It Is*, 'ruins all ages', in both English and French could mean the ruins themselves are of various vintage, or that they span all history – one manuscript of the French, where this temporal idea first comes in, gives this as 'tous les siècles' (Beckett, 2001, 478). In an extension of the rooflessness strain, this narrator a little later in the text looks at a chink of light through a hole in the door he suddenly finds himself behind, and imagines heading for the world's end, and finding himself 'between decks with the emigrants' – as though the Irish diaspora of the nineteenth century, perhaps at around the time of the Great Hunger, underscores his entire condition (115).

Ultimately, of course, after Pim, this is a tale of abandonment in which the 'I' can only counter-assert that nothing of it all had ever happened: as it says in one of the very last blocks of text, 'only me in any case alone yes' – 'no never abandoned no never was abandoned no' (193).[77] The second typescript of the French version had laid out each phrase ending 'oui' or 'non' on a separate line with a gap between the lines, as a sad and broken poetry of perfect rhymes (595–7). In a poignant reversal of Molly Bloom's final euphoria, this narrator sinks into a kind

---

[76] Laura Hensch has suggested a 'different manner of connectivity' can be detected between the blocks of text in the various parts of the novel, with the final part being the most fluid (Hensch, 2018, 298).

[77] Cordingley's conclusion that there is a kind of repeating teleology to the novel whereby the "'I'" is 'finally victorious' needs some qualification, in my view of the enduring scepticism in the latter phases: too much emphasis on the 'YES' when the 'no' is kept in play by the next instant (Cordingley, 2018, 186).

of schizophrenic isolation, deathwards progressing to no death, as Keats has it about Moneta, muse of memory.

In formal terms, Beckett of course had been experimenting with stretching and breaking syntax in blocks of text in the first five of the *Foirades/Fizzles* which date either to 1954 or 1960; he added similar experiments to the group in the late 1960s and early 1970s (Nixon, 2010, xxiv). These texts also play with exasperating readerly expectation through their extreme formal choices and disjunction. The pompous narrator of 'Horn Came Always', for example, rehearses ways to make the after-image of a face disappear, and then concludes that 'This is a help, but not a real protection, as we shall see' (142). But the text breaks off on a random image twelve lines later, and we haven't seen. It is in the large-scale fragmentation of *How It Is*, however, that Beckett stages a bewildering and intransigent and exasperating lostness for and upon the reader. The texts Cioran was accumulating across the 1960s into the early 1970s which went to make up the last part of *Le mauvais démiurge*, *Écartèlement*, and the entirety of *L'inconvenient d'être né*, the variously extensive or retracted blocks of text, were in his case often separated by asterisks or similar printer's marks. In Beckett's text, these expansions and contractions, and removed syntax which trips pattern and referent, defy consistent reading rhythm or establishment of pace in their attempt to convey the experience of disruption and diremption the voice of the text is experiencing. In this, the reader is cast adrift; the unpredictable breakings-off and leavings-short break the compact between writer and reader, at times suggest an hostility from the former to the latter.

Writerly frustration at material which refuses to find expression annoyingly becomes the reader's experience, often seemingly hitting an impasse like that of *The Unnamable*. The voice at one point in Part Two of *Comment C'est/How It Is* becomes personified, 'leaning over' as the I tries noting it all down, but getting only one word of every three or two of five:

> from age to age yes or no but above all go on impossible for the moment quite impossible that's the essential nay folly I hear it mur-mur it to the mud folly folly stop your drivel (113).

This writer enters history ('from age to age' – the French has 'de génération en génération') unable to keep pace with experience and thought. He finds it impossible for the moment to 'go on' before hitting the 'essential' that it is all 'folly' ('madness' briefly in the first English translation of 'une folie', but this is soon struck out to restore the triply repeated French term). 'Folly' is the unlikely word which will be reiterated across the halting 'What is the Word'/'Comment Dire'. It rings through *King Lear*. Kent, as early as the first scene, calls the king a majesty fallen to folly; by the fourth scene, Lear beats his skull, 'this gate that let thy folly in'. In revenge, Goneril in II.4 would have him 'taste his folly'.[78] The madness of excessiveness lurks behind all action and renders the attempt to catch up or capture in words irrelevant, as Cioran noted when titling a subsection of *Précis* 'En l'honneur de la Folie' (a subsection in which he quotes from this tragedy, as we saw earlier). Beckett's writer here commits that 'folie non-sacrée' which we also saw Cioran mulling in *La tentation*. Appropriately, Viola in Shakespeare's *Twelfth Night* reflects that 'wise men, folly-fallen, quite taint their wit'. Worstward Ho.

3.2 Beckett – Cioran – Celan

The figure of Paul Celan is encountered through Cioran's *Cahiers* in a register similar to that through which we meet Beckett there. In June 1969, for instance, Cioran records a meeting with Celan in the street at '23 heures', and a half-hour walk together, similar to those chance conversations Cioran records with Beckett. Cioran also remained acutely attentive to news about Celan, 'cet homme impossible' as he repeatedly calls him, as when Cioran is plunged into despair when walking home having heard that Celan has been forceably hospitalised following his attempt on his wife's life in early 1966 (Cioran, 1997, 326, 742).

Inevitably, things coalesce once news suddenly breaks for Cioran on 7 May 1970 that Celan has committed suicide by jumping into the Seine and when Cioran attends the funeral at the Thiais Cemetery on the edge of Paris (806–7). Later pages of *Cahiers* are threaded and punctuated with surges of memory and recognition, as well as with reflections on Celan's achievement. The absolute fact of Celan's death overwhelms Cioran as he crosses the rue Racine, and he begins to say more to himself about what made Celan 'un homme impossible' – Cioran did not particularly like him as a person ('souvent odieux' [often hateful]) but found Celan's smile the most beautiful ever seen. He must be forgiven always, given his life and woeful experience (presumably reference to the charges of plagiarism levelled at Celan from 1960, but also to Celan's parents' murders during the Second World War). And Celan was an absolute presence whose poetry could not have gone any further (807).[79]

---

[78] Frederik N. Smith reminds us that the reputed last words of Jonathan Swift were 'It is all folly.' Although restricting itself to the English literary tradition, Smith's argument for the influence of eighteenth-century writing upon Beckett has much persuasively to say about the way that that writing often defies reader expectation as it displays writerly frustration (Smith, 2002, 109). In terms which might resonate for thinking about Cioran's writing too, Smith brands *How It Is* as revealing 'a kind of decadence, appearing to be a genre wrung out at the same time that it feels like a new beginning' – and so a writing particularly appropriate to the time it was written (67).

[79] There are correlatives between Cioran's formulations as they evolve about Celan and his view of Kleist, whose work, he claimed, seemed to be 'preceded' by his suicide, rather than the other way

An evening with Celan was exhausting as you went in fear of offending him (and everything offended him, Cioran adds). Nonetheless, when attending a commemorative event for Celan at the German Centre in Paris in November 1970, Cioran comes to realise on hearing a selection of Celan's work read aloud that 'il etait hanté par les questions de langage' [it was haunted by questions about language], to obsession, to destructive limits, mournful idolisation. (We might recall that Cioran's portrait of Beckett in *Aveux* sees him as similarly obsessed.) Criticism of Celan's later work is implied here – as he listens to an actor reading Celan's poetry, Cioran seems to reflect that it fails due to the fact that Celan's wrestling with writing in German, the language of his mother but also of his parents' murderers, subsumed the work and deprived it of other facets. Notably, right after his account of this commemorative event for Celan, Cioran reports encountering Beckett in the Luxembourg, and calls him an 'homme exquis' whose presence is always beneficent – 'exquis', the word Cioran had also used to describe Celan at his best (880–1, 326). Paris for Cioran by this point has become a place of hauntings, absences, limits reached and sometimes crossed, but also of failures around the work and of sudden moments of grace too.

The missed encounter between Beckett and Celan has been mulled in Beckett studies, but, as with other aspects raised by this Element, the insertion of Cioran into the picture of Paris from the late 1940s through to the 1970s brings a slightly different tonality and inflection.[80] Celan had translated *Précis de décomposition* into German in 1953 as one of his early money-making tasks in the medium; one of Cioran's late tasks was to write a preface to a new edition of Celan's version, a preface in which he noted the violence within the uniform tone of the book, and that it represented a need to breathe, break out. Oddly, in his preface to this new edition, Cioran only mentions Celan his translator on the final page, but in telling context. Cioran seems to question the move to write in French which found its first result in *Précis*, saying that the language is too 'rigid', elegant but constraining – the 'antipodes de ma nature' [the opposite pole to my true nature] with its outbursts and angers. Yet it is a New York scholar, Erwin Chagall, who was born 'comme Paul Celan' in Czernowitz, who had

about (Cioran, 2011, 766). As Jacques Derrida points out on the basis of the opening of Celan's speech on 'The Meridian', the German poet's sense of artistic possibility was fascinated with Kleist's essay on the marionettes – that work, as we have seen via Bernold, that struck Beckett too (Derrida, 2005, 110–11). Celan's extension of his definition of art, later in his speech, to include mechanisation and a kind of robot-speech, might resonate also with 1960s Beckett texts like 'Ping'.

[80] Mark Nixon's account around Beckett and Celan remains the most comprehensive and insightful, enfolding as it does John Felstiner's and André Bernold's thoughts on the missed encounter between the two (Nixon, 2007, 152–68).

reassured him that French was paradoxically the only language in which thoughts might live (Cioran, 2011, 1246, 1249).[81]

The issue of provenance, and the connections or potential encounters built through it, together with the remote assurances it can give in alien circumstances, of course resonates across this Element. However differently inflected, and with acknowledgement of the tragic resonances of Celan's situation about this issue amidst our continuing racial prejudice, provenance binds the writings of Beckett, Cioran, and Celan as émigrés in the difficult situation of post-War Paris. Celan, who arrived and settled there in 1948, recommended the city to Ingeborg Bachmann a few years later, whilst acknowledging also that 'I had to struggle a long time before Paris accepted me properly and counted me among its own' (Bachmann and Celan, 2019, 23). And yet this understandable sensitivity towards acceptance or rejection never receded, and it configured Celan's engagement through his own writing with that of others. As John Felstiner has established, when Celan took up his situation teaching German at the École Normale Supérieure (where Beckett had taught earlier), he annually gave his students a passage from Beckett's novel *L'Innommable* to translate into German which runs partly 'And yet I am afraid, afraid of what my words will do to me, to my refuge, yet again. [. . .] If I could speak and yet say nothing, really nothing? Then I might escape being gnawed to death' (Felstiner, 2004, 38).

Celan extracted a purgatorial moment for translation (in the sentence elided by Felstiner, we are told that 'I mentioned hope, but it is not serious'). As the speaker extrapolates from these to-be-translated sentences, the text returns on itself: 'But it seems impossible to speak and yet say nothing, you think you have succeeded, but you always overlook something, a little yes, a little no' (Beckett, 2010b, 13).

Positives and negatives exchange places of signification as the self-delusion is stripped away, whilst the inevitability of speech and the desire to erase expression continue.[82] A similar mixing underwrites some of Celan's early work, as in the poem 'Sprich Auch Du' ('Speak You Too'), from *Von Schwelle zu Schwelle* (*Threshold to Threshold*) (1955). 'Sprich als letzter', the poem enjoins, speak [as/when] last; 'Sprich – | Doch scheide das Nein nicht vom Ja. | Gib deinem Spruch

---

[81] Cioran reflected further on his relationship with Celan over the translation of *Précis* in a piece published in English as 'Encounters with Paul Celan': once again he emphasises the difficulty of Celan as a man, and his vulnerability, but remarks that Celan wanted him to participate in the process of translation and discuss chapter by chapter as they emerged. Cioran felt that Celan, as a 'good translator', saw more clearly than his author (Hollander, 1988, 151).

[82] Shane Weller has comprehensively traced the doubleness of Beckett's writing towards naught and nothing, together with the philosophical tradition which underlies it (Weller, 2008, 322).

auch den Sinn' – which Pierre Joris renders 'Speak – | But do not split the No from the Yes. | Give your saying also meaning' (Celan, 2020a, 148–9).[83]

As with the use of the conjunction 'als', committed in German to the past tenses, not the present or future, there are similarly mixed perspectives to those in the passage from *The Unnamable* in Celan's poem. The injunction to speak out, to answer back, is predicated upon, as it were, being the last survivor who is indeed, as the poem progresses, increasingly denied 'refuge'. After initially witnessing that life can be glimpsed 'Beim Tode', at death, the 'you' of the poem is told that 'Nun', now, 'aber schrumpft der Ort, wo du stehst' – the place where you stand is shrinking away, and the 'you' is outcast: 'Wohin jetzt', where will you go now? The 'you' itself becomes ever the more thinned and corroded, until it is a mere gleam 'in der Dünung | wandernder Worte', which Joris gives as 'in the swell | of wandering words.'

As with the Beckett passage, the way that words stray, perhaps from the yes to the no and vice versa, or from the gleam to death, becomes the content of this Celan work in which we witness the words doing just that. Without fixed meaning, words themselves seem to erode the 'I' or the 'you'. The places upon which they might literally be grounded, in the Celan poem, are themselves forced to recede, all refuge denied. As Celan posited in an aphorism: 'On its own ruins the poem stands and hopes' (Celan, 2020b, 18). Or, in another: 'the You of the poem = (infinitely) close and infinitely far (in space and time)' (145). As 'The Meridian' speech by Celan from 1961 has it, 'Art creates I-distance. [. . .] Perhaps – I'm only asking – perhaps poetry, like art, is going with self-forgotten I toward the uncanny and the strange' (Celan, 2001, 406). This 'going', though, only furthers bewilderment – 'where?', 'in what place', 'with what?', 'as what?'. Celan's conclusion that 'poetry too hurries ahead of us at times' is provided with a sardonic gloss by Beckett's reported comment on Celan that 'Celan me dépasse', something like 'Celan's pace leaves me in the dust' (Nixon, 2007, 155).

As Celan's famous encounter with the inheritance of Hölderlin in the poem 'Tübingen, Jänner', also of 1961, confirms, this corrosion by speech and in speech is an effect, as it was for Cioran and implicitly for Beckett, of the times. Were a similar prophet to the Romantic poet who spent his later years in Tübingen to be born 'today', Celan's speaker asserts, 'er dürfte, | spräch er von dieser | Zeit, er | dürfte | nur lallen und lallen', ['he could, | were he to speak of these | days, he | could | only babble and babble'] (Celan, 2020a, 266–7). As so often in later Celan, the awkward enjambments, the stuttering repetitions of words and sounds, enact what they speak of. The split in 'von dieser | Zeit' alienates the speaker from the

---

[83] John Felstiner reads this poem as Celan encouraging himself to speak back to implied anti-Semitism in a review of his first collection, as though the history of the Holocaust might be overcome (Felstiner, 1995, 78–82).

moment as the weakness of the 'er dürfte' becomes clearer and clearer. In Cioran's entitling, this enjambment is literally a 'Fall' into time. As with Beckett's *Comment C'est/How It Is*, also from 1961, or 'Afar a Bird' from *Fizzles*, which has been dated to the same period, syntax and grammatical subordination are being strained through the formal choices made. As with the later Beckett prose, the appropriate phrase for this various estrangement is Derrida's about 'The Meridian', that it creates an 'ambiguous, even *unheimlich* grammar' (Derrida, 2005, 118). In a broken note to himself, Celan mused 'Thinker of late times /', a phrase Joris glosses via Hölderlin, and Heidegger's appropriation for his sense of belatedness of the former's 'Bread and Wine' for his own 'Dichter in dürftiger Zeit', poets in poorer times (Celan, 2020b, 88, 246).

In an odd moment amongst his notes, Celan created a web of interconnections after seeing the documentary film *Mein Kampf* by the German-Jewish film-maker Erwin Leiser. These connections take in 'the (Czernowitz native) painter Arikha' (about whom Leiser also made a film) and then Celan draws an arrow to a further note – 'Beckett+Adorno' (Celan, 2020b, 111). Once again, identification, through Avigdor Arikha, who was brought up in the same town of Celan's birth, leads to uncertainty and complexity: Celan's prolonged unhappiness at being implicated by Adorno's notorious aphorism, 'No poem after Auschwitz' (repeated in these notes; 116), shuttled via the Arikha friendship with Beckett into the whole mixture of resonances out of the film viewing itself.[84] The complexity of emotion in this aftermath of history and record presumably resonates also in the '+'. After reading Celan's 1959 collection *Sprachgitter*, Adorno concluded that only Celan stood alongside Beckett as the two authentic post-War writers (Felstiner, 1995, 107).

As with later Beckett and the contradictory late aphorisms of Cioran – and as with Celan's poetry – the issue is how to extrapolate or decipher the texts without splitting 'the No from the Yes', whilst 'signing also meaning'. Meaning is always the 'also' to one side of the text, as of its contexts. In a 1958 letter, Celan was adamant that 'what comes into language' in a poem can never be ascribed 'to something that stands outside the poem'. In the poem resides a 'quest' and the poem itself remains 'conscious enough of its own questionable beginning'. To infer anything from the poem other than the poem itself is to leave 'the domain of the concrete' and 'to distance oneself' from the poem (distance, place, 'domain', and nearness again) (Celan, 2020b, 194). In other words, as readers, we must acknowledge the 'seeking' that works inside the poem, undergo the experience of that process, but never leave the 'concrete' actuality – or find other words.

The attribution of a 'consciousness' to the poem, an awareness within of the process the words undergo from beginning to end, relates this conception to

---

[84] On Celan's continuing unhappiness about the Adorno phrase, see Felstiner (1995, 188–9).

notes that Celan made from Leibniz's *Monadology*. Posing the question to himself as to whether a poem is 'composed', Celan notes from Leibniz's text the phrase 'the compound, however, comes into being by parts, & dies away into parts'. Then we find the sequence:

> Can one <u>describe</u> a poem?
> Mirror–quality of the You –
> The process of perception – apperception in the poem. (145–6)

And, as these notes from the *Monadology* accumulate, the statement is made clearly:

> In the poem <u>something happens</u>; <u>comes to pass</u>: language as Being passes through thenarrows of the one who writes the poem: it goes through and past. (148)

The process of the poem is navigation of a kind of Scylla and Charybdis whereby the poem's own consciousness moves and shapes, comes briefly towards consciousness before fading away.

In the notes on the history of philosophy which Beckett took for himself, he was particularly concerned to copy out the Leibnizian version of perception ('the mere possession of ideas') and its difference from apperception:

> the process by which unconsciousness and confused representations are raised into conscious and clear, and so <u>appropriated by self-consciousness</u>. Genetic process of psychical life consists in the changing of unconscious into conscious presentations, in the taking up of perceptions into the clarity of self-consciousness. (Beckett, 2020, 355)[85]

Celan's related note in this regard almost echoes Beckett's source, simply replacing 'soul' with 'poem', and adding 'questionable' to 'beginning', in a further acknowledgement of the constant seeking behind the poem's 'quest': 'the soul cannot bring forth anything in its conscious ideas which has not been in it from the beginning' (356). The mirror process of the poem becomes a kind of echo chamber of identities, whereby any former idea that the reader decodes the 'meaning' of the poem in its reference to her or himself is reversed.[86] Although the poem raises itself into the 'clarity' it seeks, it does not lose connection to its inarticulate 'consciousness', what Celan calls 'the concrete.'

---

[85] Cordingley charts the significance of this understanding from Leibniz down to *Comment C'est/ How It Is* (2018, 245–58).

[86] My remarks here are inflected by a similar sense of reversal in roles mapped by Stanley Cavell's essay 'The Politics of Interpretation', although I would hesitate to affirm with him that the reversal equates to a 'freedom' for the reader. The reader, and also the writer, remain constrained by the kinds of historical conditions towards which my argument in this Element has pointed (Cavell, 1984, 52–4).

The 'niemand', the no one, found its fullest expression in the poems Celan began in 1959 and collected as *Die Niemandsrose*. It is difficult to see this 'niemand' as not (stripped of all the rhetoric around Being) that of the last of Beckett's *Texts for Nothing*: 'Whose voice, no one's, there is no one, there's a voice without a mouth, and somewhere a kind of hearing' (Beckett, 2010a, 51). 'Somewhere', not 'someone' to hear – gesture towards a space or place again in which a hearing might happen, in the absence of a proven 'one' who can listen. This is the 'niemand' of Celan's 'Psalm' – 'Ein Nichts | waren wir, sind wir, werden | wir bleiben' [Nothing we were, are, and ever more shall be] (Celan, 2020a, 264; my translation).

As Celan's translator Pierre Joris has pointed out, such growing perception as that in the 1958 letter and the notes from the *Monadology* led to a shift in Celan's practice by the early 1960s.[87] Rather than concentrating on the earlier single lyrics which are then configured like tesserae into the different sections of his books, Celan's manuscripts evidence a turn to sequences and cycles that operate 'to use a musical analogy, as sections that are *durchkomponiert*, "through-composed", and then assembled into larger coherences' (Celan, 2014, lxi).[88] As a result, the later collections become ever more diary-like, notational and spontaneous, the language ever the more neologistic or word-fractured, cut into across line endings. 'Through-composition' and abandonment seem the characteristic features too of Beckett's short prose across this period; the processes of the texts often literally embodied in the notion of setting out and pacing or walking, even where there is no setting out to be done. The opening of 'All Strange Away' – the text abandoned in early 1965 – literalises so much in the break towards new formal possibilities suggested as a shared phenomenon across the writers in this Element: 'Out of the door and down the road in the old hat and coat like after the war, no, not that again' (Beckett, 2010a, 73). 'Celan me dépasse.'

Conclusion

The turn within Beckett Studies of the past decade and more towards enquiry into Beckett's attention towards, even engagement with, his place and times opens ever new possibilities. Emilie Morin's important work demonstrates that earlier views of Beckett's career as 'divorced from recognisable political

---

[87] There are relatively few references to Leibniz in Cioran's output, although, intriguingly, in a very early discussion of how the history of philosophy has broken down utterly into 'cris', he pairs those Beckettian favourites the *Monadology* and Spinoza's *Ethics* as the texts we are to imagine as so destroyed (Cioran, 2011, 1256).

[88] Derrida sees this later work of Celan as forming a 'path' that understands its own 'privilege'; he notes its aphoristic qualities and its resistance to extrapolation: 'The certainty of a guaranteed reading would be the first inanity or the worst betrayal.' The poems are 'places' of 'unique experience' (Derrida, 2005, 129, 148).

parameters' (the view given from such as Blanchot), or that it resisted 'clear-cut referents' (as Adorno claimed), must be reviewed and reconsidered (Morin, 2017, 5). Andrew Gibson has argued that Beckett's increasing discomfort with the ways that post-War France developed across the 1950s and through the 1960s had direct resonance within the nature of his work, which adopted an increasingly 'violent aesthetic' in response (Gibson, 2010, 171). That sense of the aesthetic as being in dialogue with, developing alongside, precisely those 'referents' earlier scholars had themselves resisted is salutary – especially when taken along with Pascale Casanova's assertion that formal 'preoccupation' increasingly characterised Beckett's output (Casanova, 2006, 86). It has been the ambition of this Element to show that such contextual reading might also encompass the encounters in everyday life that a writer makes in and around the city. The lives lived are one aspect of the responses to the place and to their times, and there are consonances between writers' careers, however derived from radically different backgrounds and marked by different prior experiences they are. Those consonances, in turn, might illuminate further aspects of each writers' work as it responds to the emphases and pressures in and from 'the moment', however that moment be intellectually calibrated or configured, in art or in other aspects of system-seeking or formal creation.

The publication of Beckett's full *Philosophy Notes* shows the extent of Beckett's knowledge of the history of Western thought, a history which he clearly bore with him and which could oddly erupt through his short prose texts – as in the surprising emergence of the reference to notes on ancient Greek philosophers in 'All Strange Away' (Beckett, 2010a, 78). The glimpses afforded of his encounters with the Romanian philosopher E. M. Cioran therefore carry potential insight into the governing minutiae of Beckett's ideas, particularly into his scepticism and pessimism, attitudes, and historical emphases which are so much a characteristic of Cioran's thinking also. Cioran's sense of the twentieth century as demonstrating an ever-accelerating 'décomposition' towards 'la pire' seems echoed by that alertness to 'the chaos' which Beckett spoke of with Tom Driver, cited earlier. From the mid-1950s, Cioran was increasingly aware that this fragmentation of tradition necessitated 'briser les formes', the breaking up of the sustained surface of the (philosophical) text, as a sign of the fragmentation of ideas towards the latter part of the twentieth century.

Cioran's work, familiar from early on to Beckett and praised by him, offers a further 'take' upon its 'moment'. Cioran's arrival in Paris at the end of the War, his decision to write primarily in French, and his subsequent development of the idea of the métèque into, for good or ill, the representative figure of modern humanity, all resonate in various ways with the course Beckett's writing took after the 'siege in the room' – with its frenzy of pressuring his former aesthetic as far as it could go, before dismantling it in the short writing that began to emerge with *Textes pour rien/Texts for Nothing*. In turn also, we can see in the very different work of Paul Celan, whose ultimate origin lay in the same part of Romania as Cioran's, a similar urge to 'briser les formes' – particularly in his case after the accusations of plagiarism with which he was tragically assailed from 1960.

It will remain uncertain how far Beckett was aware of the right-wing and anti-Semitic bases for some of Cioran's later thought, or of his associations in pre-War Romania. It is unclear too how far he would have acted differently towards Cioran if he did know of them. Morin delineates eloquently the right-wing and Vichy-associated people in Paris, including Georges Pelorson/Belmont, who Beckett continued to meet and support, even once their politics and subsequent affiliations and activities were well known (Morin, 2017, 136–7). As late as 1972, Beckett could record in a letter to Bray his 'enjoyment' at reading a novel by Louis-Ferdinand Céline, long since self-unmasked as an anti-Semite Fascist sympathiser (Beckett, 2016b, 288). Perhaps, amidst so much that is imponderable, there is something to be learned in the shift Cioran made in his definition of the 'métèque' between *Précis* of 1949 and *La tentation d'exister*, 1956. The initial feverish definition of the term in a text consciously confronting the murderous fanaticism behind the recent War has, only seven years later, become a literary mask that Cioran can then deploy in his various resistance to what he continued to perceive as the cataclysmic 'fall' into ever-worsening decadence and ruin across his historical moment. It is always the strategies of the writing, the work, that prevail, as for Beckett, its shapes and forms – however those shapes and forms themselves later can come to seem symptomatic of the 'historical circumstance' from which they arise.

Cioran himself was aware that in literature, as in philosophy as so fully demonstrated in his own decomposition of his work, attention must increasingly be paid to formal and generic redundancy. *La tentation*, which contains that call 'briser', contains also an essay 'Au-dèla du roman', 'Beyond the Novel'. The essay sounds apocalypse: 'Que la littérature soit appelée à périr, c'est possible' [it is possible that literature might be called upon to cease to exist], the essay's brief final section opens – and that call might even be desirable in the current situation (Cioran, 2011, 365). Should not we all instead retool ourselves to 'une condition d'automates' – a robotic state? Arguably, Beckett's texts of the 1960s, and most directly 'Ping' and *Lessness*, approach such a 'condition' – the latter subject of a memorable consideration, for Cioran if not perhaps so deeply for Beckett, at the time of its translation. 'Au-delà du roman' pins its apocalypse figuring the end of the novel form, if not of all literature, upon the 'faillite d'une époque', the failure of the period as a whole, in which 'le *sens* commence à dater', meaning itself is beginning to date. There is an odd sense here of a corrosion or collapse of the human ability 'produire une oeuvre *qui le cachait'*, to produce a work that might conceal its creator (Cioran, 2011, 354, 361, 364).[89] Novels used to provide such concealment, yet, in the modern world, we are abandoned into the self and exposed by that abandonment as 'meaning' progressively collapses towards scepticism.

'J'ai été frappé par les affinités qui existent entre la Weltanschauung de Sam et la mienne', we find Cioran noting for himself after the Beckett evening in Paris in 1970. It is to be hoped that those 'affinités', carried through personal conversation and textual exchange, across shared world views and senses of writerly exigency in the same moment, might have become the more striking by this point.

---

[89] Derrida offers a similar sense of the modern eeriness of the date and datedness in Celan's later work in the essay 'Shibboleth' (Derrida, 2005, 5ff). Andrew Wimbush notes the similarity between Cioran's understanding of Proust and the instabilities of the self in 'Beyond the Novel' to Beckett's early essay on the French writer (Wimbush, 2020, 243, 254).

References

Ackerley, C. J., and S. E. Gontarski (2004), *The Grove Companion to Samuel Beckett*, New York: Grove Press.

Adorno, Theodor, Walter Benjamin, Ernest Bloch, Bertolt Brecht and Georg Lukàcs (1980), Aesthetics and Politic, London: Verso.

Bachmann, Ingeborg, and Paul Celan (2019), *Correspondence*, trans. Wieland Hoban, London: Seagull Books.

Badiou, Alain (2003), *On Beckett*, ed. Nina Power and Alberto Toscano, Manchester: Clinamen Press.

Beckett, Samuel, 'Sottisier' Notebook, UoR MS 2901, Beckett International Foundation, University of Reading.

Beckett, Samuel, 'Whoroscope' Notebook, UoR MS 3000, Beckett International Foundation, University of Reading.

Beckett, Samuel (1958), *Nouvelles et Texts Pour Rien*, Paris: Les Éditions de Minuit.

Beckett, Samuel (1983), *Disjecta: Miscellaneous Writings and a Dramatic Fragment*, ed. Ruby Cohn, London: Calder.

Beckett, Samuel (2001), *Comment C'est/How It Is and/et L'Image: A Critical-Genetic Edition*, ed. Édouard Magessa O'Reilly, London: Routledge.

Beckett, Samuel (2009a), *Company etc.*, ed. Dirk Van Hulle, London: Faber.

Beckett, Samuel (2009b), *Murphy*, ed. J. C. C. Mays, London: Faber.

Beckett, Samuel (2009c), *The Expelled, The Calmative, The End with First Love*, ed. Christopher Ricks, London: Faber.

Beckett, Samuel (2010a), *Texts for Nothing and Other Shorter Prose 1950–1976*, ed. Mark Nixon, London: Faber.

Beckett, Samuel (2010b), *The Unnamable*, ed. Steven Connor, London: Faber.

Beckett, Samuel (2011), *The Letters of Samuel, Beckett, Vol. II: 1941–1956*, ed. George Craig, Martha Dow Fehsenfeld, Dan Gunn, and Lois More Overbeck, Cambridge: Cambridge University Press.

Beckett, Samuel (2012), *The Collected Poems of Samuel Beckett*, ed. Séan Lawlor and John Pilling, London: Faber.

Beckett, Samuel (2014), *The Letters of Samuel Beckett, Vol. III: 1957–1965*, ed. George Craig, Martha Dow Fehsenfeld, Dan Gunn, and Lois More Overbeck, Cambridge: Cambridge University Press.

Beckett, Samuel (2016a), The Beckett Digital Library: A Digital Genetic Edition (Series 'The Beckett Digital Manuscript Project') ed. Dirk Van Hulle, Mark Nixon and Vincent Ney, Brussels: University Press Antwerp

(ASP/UPA), www.beckettarchive.org [accessed 3, 17, 24 April and 5 September 2023].

Beckett, Samuel (2016b), *The Letters of Samuel Beckett, Vol. IV: 1966–1989*, ed. George Craig, Martha Dow Fehsenfeld, Dan Gunn, and Lois More Overbeck, Cambridge: Cambridge University Press.

Beckett, Samuel (2020) *Philosophy Notes*, ed. Steven Matthews and Matthew Feldman, Oxford: Oxford University Press.

Bernold, André (2015), *Beckett's Friendship 1979–1989*, trans. Max MacGuiness, Dublin: Lilliput Press.

Boulter, Jonathan (2002), '"Wordshit, Bury Me": The Waste of Narrative in Samuel Beckett's *Texts for Nothing*', *Journal of Beckett Studies*, 11:2, pp. 1–19.

Boulter, Jonathan (2019), *Posthuman Space in Samuel Beckett's Short Prose*, Edinburgh: Edinburgh University Press. Ebook.

Branco, Daniel (2019), *Emil Cioran: The Criticism of the Idea of Historical Progress*, Melbourne: Manticore Press.

Calinescu, Martei (1996), '"How Can One Be What One Is?" Reading the Romanian and the French Cioran', *Salmagundi*, 82, Fall, pp. 192–216.

Calinescu, Martei (2002), 'The 1927 Generation in Romania: Friendships and Ideological Choices (Mihail Sebastian, Mircea Eliade, Nae Ionescu, Eugène Ionesco, E. M. Cioran)', *East European Politics and Societies*, 15:3, pp. 649–677.

Casanova, Pascale (2004), *The World Republic of Letters*, trans. M. B. DeBevoise, Cambridge, MA: Harvard University Press.

Casanova, Pascale (2006), *Samuel Beckett: Anatomy of a Literary Revolution*, London: Verso.

Cavell, Stanley (1984), *Themes Out of School: Effects and Causes*, Chicago, IL: University of Chicago Press.

Celan, Paul (2001), *Selected Poems and Prose*, trans. John Felstiner, New York: Norton.

Celan, Paul (2014), *Breathturn into Timestead: The Collected Later Poetry*, trans. Pierre Loris, New York: Farrar, Straus, Giroux.

Celan, Paul (2020a), *Memory Rose into Threshold Speech: The Collected Earlier Poetry*, trans. Pierre Loris, New York: Farrar, Straus, Giroux.

Celan, Paul (2020b), *Microliths They Are: Little Stones. Posthumous Prose*, trans. Pierre Loris, New York: Contra Mundum.

Cioran, E. M. (1968), *The Temptation to Exist*, trans. Richard Howard, introduction Susan Sontag, New York: Quadrangle.

Cioran, E. M. (1995), *Entretiens*, Paris: Gallimard.

Cioran, E. M. (1997), *Cahiers 1957–1972*, ed. Simone Boué, Paris: Gallimard.

Cioran, E. M. (2011), *Oeuvres*, ed. Nicolas Cavailès, Paris: Gallimard.

Cioran, E. M. (2012), *Drawn and Quartered*, trans. Richard Howard, New York: Arcade.

Cordingley, Anthony (2018), *Samuel Beckett's How It Is: Philosophy in Translation*, Edinburgh: Edinburgh University Press.

Cousineau, Thomas (2005), 'E. M. Cioran on Beckett', *The Beckett Circle*, 28:1, Spring, p. 5.

Cronin, Anthony (1997), *Samuel Beckett: The Last Modernist*, London: Flamingo.

David, Sylvain (2006), *Cioran: Un heroisme à rebours*, Montreal: Les Presses de l'Université de Montreal.

Davies, William (2020), *Samuel Beckett and the Second World War: Politics, Propaganda, and a 'Universe Become Provisional'*, London: Bloomsbury.

Derrida, Jacques (2005), *Sovereignties in Question: The Poetics of Paul Celan*, New York: Fordham University Press.

Farrugia, James (2015), 'Cioran's Grain of Ataraxy: Boredom, Nothingness and Quietism', *ante*, 2:3, November, pp. 207–27.

Feldman, Matthew, and Karim Mamdani, eds (2015), *Beckett/Philosophy*, Stuttgart: Ibidem-Verlag.

Feldman, Matthew, and Mark Nixon, eds (2007), *Beckett's Literary Legacies*, Cambridge: Cambridge Scholar.

Felstiner, John (1995), *Paul Celan: Poet. Survivor. Jew*, Yale, CT: Yale University Press.

Felstiner, John (2004), 'Samuel Beckett Meets Paul Celan', *American Poetry Review*, 33:4, July–August, p. 38.

Gibson, Andrew (2010), *Samuel Beckett*, London: Reaktion.

Graver, Lawrence, and Raymond Graver, eds (1979), *Samuel Beckett: The Critical Heritage*, London: Routledge.

Hensch, Laura (2018), '"Torn by Enormous Pauses": Counter-Rhythmic Caesurae in *How It Is*', *Samuel Beckett Today/Aujourd'hui*, 30:2, pp. 291–304.

Hollander, Benjamin, ed. (1988), 'Translating Tradition: Paul Celan in France', *Acts*, 8/9, pp. 151–2.

Hui, Andrew (2019), *A Theory of the Aphorism*, Princeton, NJ: Princeton University Press.

Joubert, Claire (2012), 'Badiou with Beckett: Concept, Prose, and the Poetics 'de l'avenir', *Journal of Beckett Studies*, 21:1, pp. 33–60.

Juliet, Charles (2009), *Conversations with Samuel Beckett and Bram Van Velde*, trans. Tracy Cooke and Axel Nesme, Champaign, IL: Dalkey Archive.

Keatinge, Benjamin (2013), 'Samuel Beckett and Emil Cioran: Towards a Comparative Analysis', *New Europe College Yearbook 2014–15*, pp. 155–77.

Knowlson, James (1996), *Damned to Fame: The Life of Samuel Beckett*, London: Bloomsbury.

Morin, Emilie (2017), *Beckett's Political Imagination*, Cambridge: Cambridge University Press.

Nadeau, Maurice (1990), *Grâces leurs soient rendres*, Paris: Éditions Albin Michel.

Nixon, Mark (2006), '"Scraps of German": Beckett Reading German Literature', *Samuel Beckett Today/Aujourd'hui*, 16, pp. 259–82.

Nixon, Mark (2007), '"Text-Void": Silent Words in Paul Celan and Samuel Beckett', in Matthew Feldman and Mark Nixon (eds), *Beckett's Literary Legacies*, Newcastle: Cambridge Scholars, pp. 152–68.

Nixon, Mark (2010), 'Preface', in Samuel Beckett, *Texts for Nothing and Other Shorter Prose 1950–1976*, ed. Mark Nixon, London: Faber, pp. vii–xxiv.

Noiriel, Gérard (2007), *Immigration, Anti-Semitisme et Racisme en France XIXe e XXe Siècle: Discours Publics, Humiliations Privées*, Paris: Hachette.

Oprescu, Florian (2013), 'E. M. Cioran and the Self-Image of the Modern Philosopher in the Broken Mirror', *Procedia: Social and Behavioral Sciences*, 71, pp. 182–8.

O'Reilly, Édouard Magessa (2001), 'English Introduction', in Samuel Beckett, *Comment C'est/How It Is and/et L'Image: A Critical-Genetic Edition*, ed. Édouard Magessa O'Reilly, London: Routledge, pp. ix–xxxvi.

Pazan, Michael (2004), *'L'écriture génocidaire': Anti-Semitisme en style et discours*, Paris: Calmann-Lévy.

Pilling, John (1977), 'Two Versions of De-composition: Samuel Beckett and E. M. Cioran', *NVQ*, Summer, pp. 305–14.

Pilling, John (1979), 'E. M. Cioran: An Introduction', *PN Review*, 6:1, pp. 14–17.

Platon, Mircea (2012), '"The Iron Guard" and the "Modern State": Iron Guard Leaders Vasile Marin and Ion I. Moța, and the "New European Order"', *Fascism*, 1, pp. 65–99.

Pope, Alexander (1993), *The Major Works*, ed. Pat Rogers, Oxford: Oxford University Press.

Rabaté, Jean-Michel (2016), 'Excuse My French: Samuel Beckett's Style of No Style', *CR: The New Centennial Review*, 16:3, Winter, pp. 133–49.

Regier, Willis G. (2005), 'Cioran's Nietzsche', *French Forum*, 30:3, Fall, pp. 75–90.

Smith, Frederik N. (2002), *Beckett's Eighteenth Century*, London: Palgrave.

Sontag, Susan (1969), *Styles of Radical Will*, New York: Farrar, Straus and Giroux.

Swift, Jonathan (1976), Gulliver's Travels *and Other Writings*, ed. Louis A. Landa, Oxford: Oxford University Press.

Van Hulle, Dirk, and Mark Nixon (2013), *Samuel Beckett's Library*, Cambridge: Cambridge University Press.

Weller, Shane (2008), '"Gnawing to Be Naught": Beckett and Pre-Socratic Nihilism', *Samuel Beckett Today/Aujourd'hui*, 20, Amsterdam: Rodopi, pp. 321–33.

Weller, Shane (2013), 'Post World-War Two Paris', in Anthony Uhlmann (ed.), *Samuel Beckett in Context*, Cambridge: Cambridge University Press, pp. 160–72.

Weller, Shane (2021), *Samuel Beckett and Cultural Nationalism*, Cambridge: Cambridge University Press.

Wheatley, David (2013), '"Sweet Thing Theology": Beckett, E. M. Cioran and the Lives of the Saints', in Peter Fifield and David Addyman (eds), *Samuel Beckett: Debts and Legacies. New Critical Essays*, London: Bloomsbury, pp. 39–62.

Whitehead, David (1977), *The Ideology of the Athenian Metic*, Cambridge: Cambridge Philological Society.

Wimbush, Andy (2020), *Still: Samuel Beckett's Quietism*, Stuttgart: Ibidem.

Zarifopol-Johnston, Ilina (2007), 'Found in Translation: The Two Lives of E. M. Cioran, or How Can One Be a Comparatist?' *Comparative Literature Studies*, 44:1–2, pp. 20–37.

Zarifopol-Johnston, Ilinca (2009), *Searching for Cioran*, ed. Kenneth R. Johnston, Bloomington: Indiana University Press.

Cambridge Elements ☰

Beckett Studies

Dirk Van Hulle
University of Oxford

Dirk Van Hulle is Professor of Bibliography and Modern Book History at the University of Oxford and director of the Centre for Manuscript Genetics at the University of Antwerp.

Mark Nixon
University of Reading

Mark Nixon is Associate Professor in Modern Literature at the University of Reading and the Co-Director of the Beckett International Foundation.

About the Series

This series presents cutting-edge research by distinguished and emerging scholars, providing space for the most relevant debates informing Beckett studies as well as neglected aspects of his work. In times of technological development, religious radicalism, unprecedented migration, gender fluidity, environmental and social crisis, Beckett's works find increased resonance. Cambridge Elements in Beckett Studies is a key resource for readers interested in the current state of the field.

Cambridge Elements ☰

Beckett Studies

Printed in the United States
by Baker & Taylor Publisher Services